A Thought for Your Pennies

Ken Morris

Table of Contents

Introduction

"Thoughts For Your Pennies" is a collection of my columns from the pages of The Oakland Press. For two decades, I've enjoyed sharing thoughts and ideas with my readers. The columns I've selected are some of my favorites. I hope you enjoy them.

Here's how it all started.

Some twenty years ago, my local newspaper published an article about my financial planning firm and me. During the interview they asked what I thought about their expanded Sunday Business Section. I politely told them that I didn't think it was very good.

A week or so later, they called and asked if I thought I could do better. Although I had no formal training in writing, I said yes.

So they offered me a four-week trial to write their Sunday Business column. Today, with more than 700 columns published, I'm still going strong, every Sunday.

Much has happened in the world of finance over the past twenty years. In 1999, the maximum contribution into an IRA was $2,000. Currently, it's $6,000, plus an additional $1,000 if you're over 50. The maximum contribution into a 401(k) in 1999 was $10,000. Today, it's $19,000, again, with additional deposits allowed for those 50 or older. The Dow Jones Industrial Average closed the year at 11,497 in 1999. It's near 26,000 today.

I mention these numbers to highlight how much government

rules and tax laws have changed over the years. And though they may change frequently, the need for good advice never changes. And that's something I hope my readers have found in the words of my columns.

I've guided my clients and readers through many peaks and valleys, including the Great Recession of 2008. I've helped many of them work toward their financial goals and dreams, from building a retirement nest egg to funding a loved one's college education.

I'm not patting myself on the back; I simply want to share with you some of the simple, yet overlooked strategies that are needed when working toward your financial objectives. This book is not heavy with boring financial jargon. Rather, it's full of common sense, something often overlooked when handling money. I want this book to be easy to read and full of meaningful messages you can share with your friends and family.

I'd be remiss if I didn't thank my friend and editor John Altomare, also known as Doctor Rock for his knowledge of rock and roll oldies, including the flip sides of many hits. Finally, I thank my broker/dealer, LPL Financial. Every week, before my columns hit the newspaper, they are reviewed to comply with current policies as well as current regulatory standards by the LPL Financial compliance department. I appreciate their prompt attention and their efforts to help me publish this book.

Ken Morris
2019

CHAPTER 1

Just you wait until your father comes home.

Ken Morris
As seen in the Oakland Press
3-8-09

Goals can be accomplished regardless of age.

Every year around this time, I attend an educational workshop with many of my peers from throughout the country. The workshops have always been beneficial for me because I often pick up thoughts and ideas from other advisors or featured speakers, usually economists. I feel it's helped me to be a better financial advisor.

This year was somewhat different in that so many advisors, like much of the general public, were mentally down. As you might expect, a great deal of the talk was negative, but surprisingly, some of the economic news presented was cautiously optimistic.

I shared a personal story with some of my colleagues who thought it was the most uplifting story they had heard in some time. Even though it doesn't specifically involve personal finance, many encouraged me to share it with my readers because they felt it was both uplifting and illustrative of how people can truly help and succeed in times of difficulty.

The story involves my family, specifically my father, who lost his parents at a fairly young age. At that time, there weren't the kinds of social services programs we have today. A family in their early thirties with children of their own took him in. There was no monthly check to help the family raise him. He was an extra mouth to feed during a time when the economy was struggling. My father had to work for his keep. The family that took him in ran a John Deere store.

My father recalls weighing 100 pounds and having to move and stack 100-pound sacks at this country store. It was indeed tough love and hard work, but it taught him something that I believe many people are lacking today. A strong work ethic.

Over the years, I know my dad gave his best. He lived the ethic that he taught all his children, that the only effort good enough is your best effort.

As mentioned, economic times were tough back then, and my father had enlisted in the service after the 11th grade. Upon returning home from the service, he married, raised a family and worked hard to support all his kids. I knew the family that took him in as grandma and grandpa. There was never any question that they were my family. They helped raise him because they cared. Sadly, we just buried grandpa a few weeks ago.

Like so many people raising a family, dad's life was busy. Over the years, he worked hard and eventually became manager of a large, well- respected car dealership. That was when American cars were in their heyday, so dad worked a lot of hours. His efforts fed us, housed us and helped educate us all. But my dad always felt he was lacking something in life -- a high school diploma.

Dad will turn 80 in a couple of months. But a few weeks ago, he received his high school diploma from the Ann Arbor school district. For once it was the kids beaming with pride for their dad.

In this day and age, when it seems like all the news is depressing, I thought I would share a positive, uplifting story with my readers. Along with the lesson that goals can be accomplished regardless of age.

Ken Morris
As seen in Oakland Press 6/16/13

Make your money last as long as you're breathing.

A person who probably had a significant impact on your financial attitudes and outlook is your father. If he was a part of your life, your dad likely played a major role in forming your view of finances. He may have taught you directly or you may have formed them by following his example. In other words, he taught you indirectly.

As with family values, financial values tend to be passed along. Dads have an inherent knack for teaching the importance of a dollar, how to save money and how to spend it.

For example, at one time or another, most of us heard our father say, "We can't afford it." It may have been the hard truth or, perhaps, just a teaching moment. Whatever the case, it helped us learn the value of money.

Many fathers of the World War II generation never attended college. But we've all heard stories of dads who put in countless hours at work in order to save money to send their sons or daughters to college. No sacrifice was too great for them to provide their children with the education that had eluded them

Think about it. During the course of your "growing up," wasn't it often your dad and his views on money and finances that helped mold your viewpoint on money related issues? As a financial advisor, I think that a father's role on teaching the kids finances is often overlooked and seldom discussed. But it should be.

Speaking for myself, I have been blessed with a dad that has always been a huge part of my life. And I feel fortunate just for that fact alone, never mind all the things I learned from him.

I know the world has changed significantly since my formative years. I'm aware that the traditional role of the father has diminished, but I believe more than ever that a positive father's role is vitally important. And not just for teaching pocketbook issues.

In no way am I trying to diminish or minimize the importance of other influences in life, especially mothers, teachers and peers. But on some occasions I think society minimizes the importance of being a good father.

On a personal note, I have reached the stage in life where I am attending a lot of weddings for both family and friends. It's nice to see so many young adults launch their lives together.

Yet I have little doubt that these young adults will have to deal with important financial issues in the years ahead. There will be a lot of questions. They may be regarding the purchase of a first home, or a mortgage refinance. They may be about how to how to establish a college fund for a newborn or save for retirement. But they most certainly will be.

I'm hopeful that they will turn to dad for help with answering these questions, and equally hopefully that all you dads can be as helpful to your kids as your dad was for you.

I may be biased, but I believe a good father can and should help with a lot of issues, including financially related ones. And on that note, I'd like to wish my father and all the fathers out there a Happy Father's Day.

Ken Morris
As seen in Oakland Press 4/6/14

The rewards and obligations of a Financial Advisor.

I've been fortunate in that I have several clients that have been with me for over twenty years. They've not only entrusted me with their financial well being, they've also shared pictures and stories of important life events, like weddings and the birth of grandchildren.

To a certain extent we have grown together. From a financial perspective, at least, I've helped them navigate life's journeys. It's been difficult at times, but if I had to do it all over again, I would choose the exact same path that brought me to where I am today.

For me, the personal satisfaction of helping people achieve their financial goals far exceeds any difficulties along the way.

I mention this because, when you see people on a regular basis, the relationship often becomes more than just business. And while illness or death can change the dynamic of any relationship, there's another circumstance that almost always causes the relationship to evolve. People get older.

When you see clients over time, you can sense and feel when the aging process starts to catch up with them. That's when a financial advisor, or any professional for that matter, needs to go the extra mile. Beyond just guiding and advising, I believe it's equally important to be protective of them.

My own parents are a good example of the effects of aging. Recently, there was a billing issue with an insurance premium. In years past, it would have just been a minor problem for them to solve. But today, with time on their hands, it became a stressful issue. I believe this is typical. Such issues tend to be a bit larger and a more problematic for aging people.

My father's dentist is a good example of a professional going the extra mile to accommodate an aging person. Sensitive to ongoing health issues, he provided pillows and blankets for my father while in the dentist's chair.

One big reason why financial advisors need to be extra protective of aging clients is their vulnerability. There are so many financial predators out there who try to take advantage of seniors. I recently came across an elderly person who was "talked into" liquidating a conservative and relatively secure account to invest it in a rather speculative investment. A move that made no sense to me.

People over the age of 70 are aware of required minimum distributions. I've had clients claim they never took one when I knew for certain that they had. On one occasion, an elderly client claimed that someone had stolen the check from her mailbox and cashed it. My staff ultimately determined that the she deposited the check and had simply forgotten about it.

Why are senior clients so vulnerable? Sadly, I've seen many instances where it's simply because they're not as mentally sharp as in years past. As a financial advisor who works with many senior clients, I believe it's imperative that all advisors provide conscientious and patient service to our aging client base.

My experience is that seniors rarely demand or even expect special attention. Maybe they're too proud, but I believe they've earned the right and deserve to get it. They shouldn't have to worry about unscrupulous individuals trying to take advantage of the wealth that they've amassed.

Ken Morris
As seen in Oakland Press 6/15/14

My first Father's Day without my father.

A person who probably had a significant impact on your financial attitudes and outlook is your father. If he was a part of your life, your dad likely played a major role in molding your views of the world, including finances. He may have taught you directly or perhaps you learned indirectly, by following his example

Just as with family values, financial values tend to be passed along. Dads have an inherent knack for teaching the importance of money, how to save it and how to spend it.

For example, at one time or another, most of us heard our father say, "We can't afford it." Whether it was the hard truth or just a teaching moment, it helped us learn the value of money.

Many fathers of the World War II generation never attended college. But how many stories have you heard about dads who worked countless hours in order to save money to send their sons or daughters to college. No sacrifice was too great for them to provide their children with the education they never had.

Think about it. During the course of growing up, wasn't it your dad's views on money and finances that helped mold yours? As a financial advisor, I believe the father's role in teaching the kids finances is seldom discussed. But it should be.

I was blessed with a dad that played a huge role in my life. And I feel fortunate just for that, let alone all he taught me. My father recently passed away, but I continue to carry his wisdom with me every day.

I know the world has changed significantly since my formative years. I'm aware the traditional role of the father has diminished. But now that my father is gone, it's become apparent to me that that a positive father's role is more important now than ever. And not just for teaching pocketbook issues.

Don't misunderstand. I'm not diminishing the importance of other influences in life, particularly mothers, teachers and peers. But sometimes I think society does minimize the importance of being a good father.

Keeping it personal, I've reached the stage in life where I'm attending a lot of weddings, most recently those of my niece and middle son. It's very rewarding to see young adults launch their lives together.

Yet I have little doubt that these young adults will have to deal with important financial issues in the years ahead. There will be a lot of questions. They may be about purchasing a first home, or refinancing a mortgage. Or perhaps about establishing a child's college fund or saving for retirement. But there most certainly will be questions.

I'm hopeful that they'll turn to dad to help with the answers, and equally hopeful that every dad out there can be as helpful to your kids as your dad was for you.

I may be biased, but I believe a good father can and should help his children with a lot of issues, including financially related ones.

I miss my father, and I will never forget him. I urge everyone to take a moment, in thought or in person, to thank your dad for all he's done for you. And I wish every dad a Happy Father's Day.

Ken Morris
As seen in Oakland Press 6/18/17

My father taught me what Uncle Sam can't.

It's hard for me to believe it's already Father's Day. Stating the obvious, it means the year is almost half over. From a financial perspective, I learned a great deal from my dad regarding many aspects of life, but especially money related issues.

I saw how hard he worked, how generous he was with friends, how much repeat business he did with his customers. But most important to me was how he always put family first. In hindsight, I'm fairly certain he shielded my siblings and me from his financial concerns. Isn't that what most dads do?

Looking back, the lessons I learned from my dad molded me into the person I am today. As a boy, I remember when life in general was much simpler than it is today. Time moved at a much slower pace, problems were far less complex and the world felt much safer.

Perhaps I was shielded from reality, but I will always look back with fond memories and sincere appreciation for what my dad and mom taught me.

If my father were still alive, he would be stunned that there are so many mandatory ethics classes in my field. Ethics are something that parents help mold while you're growing up. I can't imagine an adult changing his or her behavior with a client because of something they learned in an ethics class. I firmly believe that by the time you're an adult you are what you are.

Now there are brand new Department of Labor rules that mandate financial advisors put their clients' interests ahead of their own. Again, I doubt that the new regulations will change the mindset of most advisors.

I believe the vast majority of advisors already try to do the best they can for their clients. I look at my office and, other than increasing the amount of paperwork and adding to the complexity of an already complex business, very little will change.

If you're already acting in the best interest of clients, nothing ultimately needs to be changed other than the new forms that will needed to be completed and signed.

It all comes back to how you were molded as a child. If you were taught to know right from wrong, I don't believe ethics training and regulations are really necessary.

If you're an honest businessperson you don't need a government agency to tell you how to be one. Instead of having more government regulations telling us what to do, we need more moms and dads to set the standards- in both our daily lives and in the business world.

When parents set the moral compass for their children, they know what to do. It's second nature. Honesty and ethical behavior can be legislated, but it can't be taught by regulation.

Father's Day is a time for fond reflections of the past. But it's also a day for the dads of the world to step up and make certain that they're positive role models for their sons, daughters and grandchildren.

A day doesn't go by that I don't thank my dad for showing me the way, simply by watching how he treated people. I hope I'm doing the same for my sons.

And on that note, Happy Father's Day to every dad out there.

Ken Morris
As seen in Oakland Press 5/13/18

This day isn't just for mothers. It's for motherhood.

It may sound funny, but there aren't too many people in the world that I'd like to change places with. I have an enjoyable career and a loving family that puts up with me and my silly humor.

Of course there have been difficult days, but most of the time life is pretty darn good. Many people work their entire lives, then retire and seek a job or passion they enjoy.

I'm fortunate in that I've been living that feeling for years. Today, on Mother's Day, I tip my hat to the wonderful women in my life.

I've been blessed with a strong and supportive wife. In those rare instances when I'm down, she makes certain I got back on track. Early in my career, when we were building our firm, she never complained about the long hours away from home and the unpredictable income.

It was difficult with three young boys, but she made certain they were well behaved and studied hard for school. I could just come home and play with the boys, but she did most of the difficult tasks.

Those young boys grew up and today they've brought some wonderful young ladies in our family. All are great examples of working women who multi-task a career and motherhood.

The women at my office also pour their hearts and souls into making certain all is in good order for our clients. They understand how important our clients are, and are equally proficient at keeping their own households in good order.

I know because I've been there, and watched their families blossom. I've enjoyed going to their children's graduations, and I'll soon be attending my assistant's daughter's wedding. In short, I've been very fortunate in that outstanding women surround me in both my personal life and at the office.

Over the years of working with families, I've tried to emphasize the importance of both spouses having a firm grasp of the family finances. That's because at some point in life, hopefully after years of marriage, it's quite likely that one spouse will be handing all the money.

It's not a male or female thing, but more often than not, I find that one spouse is more financially engaged than the other. The ultimate financial scenario will be much more manageable if both spouses are involved and working toward a unified goal.

Getting the children involved can also be beneficial. One way is to teach them the importance of saving early. For example, my son, who is also a financial advisor, and his wife keep a piggy bank handy for their two-year-old son, who really enjoys dropping coins into that bank.

Recently, he and his parents went to great grandma's house to celebrate his second birthday. How fortuitous it was that he brought his piggy bank with him.

But when great grandma gave him a $5 bill, my grandson had no interest. It was far more fun to pick up pennies and drop them into the bank! Fortunately, great grandma just happened to have a handful of coins at the ready.

On that note, I want to thank all the caring and generous mothers in my life. I hope that they and all the other mothers out there have a very, very special day.

CHAPTER 2

That and three dollars will buy you a cup of coffee.

Ken Morris
As seen in the Oakland Press
2-15-09

Why relationships can fail when the market falls.

For many readers, yesterday was a night on the town, a day for candy, flowers and dining out. Valentine's Day is traditionally a day when couples reaffirm their love and commitment to one another. However, I suggest that it's not a day on which couples should discuss finances. Because talking about money issues on Valentine's Day is like throwing a bucket of water on a fire. In other words, it will quickly put out the flame.

It is no secret that finances are at the root of many couples' problems. Financial issues have doomed many marriages. Arguments over who spends how much and what they buy are often the culprits that cause a marriage to fail. Obviously, many marriages do survive such issues, but money matters can still contribute to significant stress.

In the current economic situation, finances have to be affecting far more relationships than they normally would. Home values, which everyone seemed to believe would only go up and up into the future, have plummeted.

Funds that had been set aside for kids' college education are no longer making the grade. Retirement nest eggs look like they have been picked over by ravenous vultures. In fact, the net worth of many families has fallen so precipitously that, financially, it looks like they *did* go through a divorce.

Our current economic downturn has altered almost everyone's plans in some way or other. Many people lost their job unexpectedly. Some were forced to retire far earlier than they had planned, and many of them are just hanging on financially by a thread. The world has changed suddenly and dramatically.

It seems like it was last September, when Lehman Brothers failed, that the dominoes really began to fall. Another sign the world has changed is reflected in a recent survey that I came across conducted by Sun Life Financial. Sun Life is a highly rated, well-respected insurance and investment company. I take their work very seriously.

As you are probably aware, there are indices that measure virtually anything and everything. For example, investors are likely familiar with the Standard & Poor's 500 index, a tool that measures the daily ups and downs of the broader stock market. Then there are indices that measure consumer confidence, like the one published by the University of Michigan.

Now, Sun Life has introduced something totally new; something that I believe is a good indication of the times we live in. They have developed the Unretirement Index, which gauges how economic and financial forces impact American workers.

I was specifically interested the findings of their recent survey that tracked the attitudes and expectations of workers who work at least 20 hours per week after they reach the age when they become eligible to receive Social Security benefits.

In a nutshell, the survey indicated that 54% of such workers plan to delay their retirement date by at least a year. Nearly one in four of those surveyed said that they would likely have to work five years more than initially anticipated. All as a result of this recent economic crisis.

The bottom line is quite clear. Financial issues and concerns can have an enormous impact on personal relationships. That's why financial communication and understanding are critical for building a successful, long-lasting relationship.

Ken Morris
As seen in The Oakland Press 7/25/10

Parents should be good financial role models for their children.

Some clients recently mentioned to me that they are concerned about their children's future. Specifically, they're worried about the financial wellbeing of their children. Now that, in and of itself, is not unusual. But what is somewhat surprising is that my clients children are well into their forties.

It really got me to thinking. As parents, are we doing enough to educate our children in the economic basics they will need throughout their lives? I'm not really sure.

Although my children are significantly younger and just launching their careers, I worry about their finances too. Obviously, from when they are infants, we try to teach them right from wrong, and instill in them proper manners and respect for their peers and adults.

In addition to teaching them all these things and more, a great deal of knowledge and behavior is passed on to them by parental example. So I want you to ask yourself if you are or have been a good financial model for your children.

Finance and investing are not events; they are ongoing, evolving processes that change, day in and day out. That's why I believe, as parents, there is no end to the opportunities you have to teach or lead by example, regardless of the age of your children.

For example, anything from mortgage rates to investments can and should be part of the family discussion. And, regardless of how old they are or where they may be living, I'm fairly certain your children are at least somewhat aware of how you handle money. Quite possibly, keenly aware.

The 2009 Charles Schwab Parents & Money Survey had a number of interesting tidbits of information. A couple of highlights jumped out at me. First is that 27 percent of those surveyed believed the best way to learn about money is through parental example. And second, 44 percent believed guided, hands-on experience was the best way to learn.

So the question emerges again. As parents, are we actively guiding, or are we too passive in teaching our children?

There's no question that many families are struggling to make ends meet. In years past, clients would periodically come in and withdraw a respectable amount from their nest egg to buy that Florida vacation home they fell in love with during the winters.

Those days appear to be long gone. In today's world, my clients come in and take a sizeable withdrawal from their nest egg to help their adult age sons or daughters.

I can certainly understand helping family. However, what concerns me a bit is that, more often than not, mom and dad could have or should have seen it coming.

They should have noticed if their children were being too nonchalant with their money and making poor money decisions. When I ask if they ever spoke to their kids about poor money management, the most common response is, they never felt it was any of their business.

Wrong! Your children's finances are always your business. As parents, you are the bank of last resort. You're never too old to teach and lead by example. Being a good financial role model will also help minimize the risk of becoming a "club famwich," which is slang for multiple generations living in the same house.

Ken Morris
As seen in The Oakland Press 10/31/10

Halloween horrors come once a year,
but financial horrors can interrupt your life.

In just a few days, we will once again be able to turn on our television sets without being bombarded by political advertisements.

If you turned on the tube for something other than the news or a football game, there's a good chance you caught one of the plethora of Halloween horror movies that have been airing lately.

Right now, I can't say what's more frightening, a movie with a horrific looking creature carrying a chainsaw or a politician during the commercial break trying to make his opponent look scarier than the chainsaw wielder.

As adults, we know that the movie is pure fiction. We also should be aware that politicians are not above stretching the truth as far as humanly possible to put themselves in a better light than their opponent. We just have to accept that both types of fiction, Dracula movies and political campaigns, are a part of the fabric of our country.

This time of year also brings us the tradition of taking the kids trick or treating. When my children were young, I enjoyed taking them through the neighborhood. It was fun to see the neighbors and their kids, decked out in their costumes.

The day after Halloween, television programming tends to get back to normal, and a few days later after the election, the winning politician will tell us the opponent that he or she previously vilified is not such a bad person.

So, before you know it, all the scary movies and political ads will be things of the past, at least for another year. We knew the horror movies weren't real. And even though we may not agree with the winning politicians' views or policies, we may actually come to find that they're really not as scary as portrayed.

But, that doesn't mean that real horror can't interrupt your life. Some terrible things are for real. I mean what if you suddenly and unexpectedly passed away? A terrible thought, indeed, but it does happen. We read about it in the newspaper or see it on the news almost every day.

I'm real concerned because I constantly discuss the importance of saving and investing. But it's also important to protect your most important asset, human capital. Unfortunately, not enough people are protecting their families, leaving them exposed to the real life horror and possible financial hardship of the loss of a loved one.

A recent study by the Life Insurance Marketing and Research Association (LIMRA) found that the number of people owning life insurance hit a 50 year low. Only 44 percent of households in the country currently own individual life insurance.

Now that's really scary. I know that many families are hurting financially, but too many are cutting back and leaving their families in an extremely vulnerable situation.

Basic financial planning preaches protecting your potential liabilities prior to taking on additional risk. The LIMRA study shows most households are not doing this, which is a real concern.

The horrors of Halloween are once a year. The horrors of losing a family member are forever and likely to be financially devastating. It's time to review your life insurance policies with your life agent. And if you don't have a policy or an agent, it's time to find one.

Ken Morris
As seen in The Oakland Press 3/4/12

Spend your bonus checks wisely.

For whatever reason, I have difficulty reading while flying. So, on my most recent trip I decided to watch a movie on my laptop. So as not to offend any casual onlookers, I watched Dolphin Tale, a Disney movie based on a true story.

I can honestly say it made the flight seem faster and I enjoyed the movie, about a young boy being raised by his single mother. When the boy's cousin was about to enter the military, he gave the young boy a pocket-sized multi-function tool as a going away present.

Shortly thereafter, on the way to school, the boy stumbled across a beached dolphin. He used his multi-tool's blade to help free the dolphin from the nets in which he was entangled. The storyline went on about the boy and the dolphin and it was quite inspirational.

So why do I mention this in a financial column?

Perhaps I'm somewhat frustrated by the ever-changing onslaught of regulations in the financial services industry. But, my first reaction to this wonderful movie was that if it happened locally, it would be front-page news for all the wrong reasons.

First, the boy would have been banned from school indefinitely for bringing a knife blade to school. Second, the hard-working mother's ability to raise her son would have been carefully scrutinized. In the movie, of course, the young boy saved the dolphin and was a hero.

I'm not by any means suggesting it's okay to bring a knife to school. However, I would like to point out that common sense and the ability to think on your own appears to have taken a back seat to an abundance of rules and regulations.

The securities industry, banking and manufacturing have all expressed frustration over the difficulty of complying with an ever-increasing number of regulations. In the financial services industry, they are more stringent that at any time in my career. Sometimes I wonder if regulations have superseded the ability to think on one's own.

That being said, I believe that no matter how strict the regulations, there will always be a criminal element trying to sidestep the rules for personal gain.

Many experts believe the "next" financial crisis will be the college loan debacle. Some say it will dwarf the recent mortgage crisis, while others are calling for more regulation.

Before we blame those who provided the loans or rush to add more regulations, I believe we should focus on better educating our young adults about finances.

Let's teach them the math of borrowing money, whether for school, a credit card or a mortgage. Before the debate over the cause of the student loan crisis escalates, I question how many really understand the mathematics of what it takes to pay back a six-figure student loan.

Today's reality is that not many college grads are going to land a job at the top of the wage scale. This makes paying back debt even more difficult over one's working career. At all stages of life, people need the mathematical ability to get through the business of life.

Clearly, every situation and circumstance cannot be perfectly regulated. But, there has to be room for individual common sense and time to think through an issue or problem. No amount of regulation can assure that everyone's life is a Disney movie with a happy ending.

Ken Morris
As seen in The Oakland Press 11/11/12

You are responsible for your own financial future.

All the political advertisements have finally ended. From national to local levels, positions have been filled and propositions have been passed or killed. And the courting for your vote is over. It was quite an assault of questionable claims, innuendoes and perhaps even intentional misinformation. But it's over.

I think the only blessing that came from that bombardment of political ads was the fact that they overshadowed the corporate earnings season reports and forecasts.

In case you haven't been paying attention to corporate earnings lately, they haven't been much to write home about. I don't believe it would be far off to say that, overall, the earnings reports are forecasting an outlook that's more pessimistic than optimistic.

At the end of the day, after all of the political promises and all of the business and economic forecasts, you have to ask yourself who is responsible for your financial future. The answer, of course, is you are.

Regardless of how you view the political results, most readers still have the same concerns today as they did prior to entering the voting booth. Election results don't change the fact that next month there will still be bills to pay and mouths to feed.

That being said, recent research has indicated that many families are carrying their responsibilities and concerns well beyond the traditional post education years.

We all know that the new health care law allows families to maintain their children on their health care coverage until the age of 26. Although the intent may be noble and the action necessary, I find this course of events a bit disturbing.

My concern is and always has been that the longer we tend to shelter our young adults from the reality of the costs of the real world, the more we may be providing them a disservice in the long run.

A recent report from the National Center for Policy Analysis essentially confirms that my concerns have some validity. Some of their findings are real eye openers; even more surprising than I had expected.

The report shows that 59 percent of parents are providing financial support to their children between the ages of 18 and 39 who are no longer in school. (No, 39 is not a misprint.) Additionally, 48 percent of parents are assisting with day-to-day living expenses for this same age group.

Also, a whopping 29 percent are doling out spending money.

I could go on, but it's a clear trend that parents are financially helping their children well beyond age 26.

Obviously, there are a number of contributing factors involved, but parents today are clearly carrying their economic responsibilities well beyond the traditional age of adulthood.

This is not a criticism, just a lament that it's become necessary and is so prevalent. Because there's another aspect to the situation that's worrisome.

If parents are stepping in and helping out their children well into their thirties, you have to wonder if they're putting their own financial security in retirement at risk.

Is the job market so discombobulated that our children will never become financially independent? Is our economy far weaker than anyone is willing to admit? I can't definitively answer those questions, but I can tell you who is responsible for your financial future.

You are.

Ken Morris
As seen in Oakland Press 6/2/13

There's nothing routine about assisting aging parents.

Just prior to the Memorial Day holiday, one of my clients, a career military professional, returned home to help take care of his ailing father. Without going into personal details, he indicated that there are a lot of people overseas just like him that are worried about aging parents.

Ironic, isn't it? While we're here at home worried about the safety of our loved ones as they put themselves in harms way, they are over there equally concerned about aging parents.

While the world may be getting smaller, in many ways it's also becoming increasingly complex. And that complexity often necessitates dramatic changes in routine.

For example, not that many years ago when I opened a new account for a client, I had to obtain routine information that could be completed on one page. It's certainly not that way any more. Nowadays, when I complete the forms for a new client, the stack of papers is as thick as a small town telephone book.

Such complexity is not unique to the financial services field. It has touched almost all aspects of our society, including what needs to be done when it's time to help our aging parents.

Assisting aging parents might entail meetings with lawyers, accountants, senior housing administrators and, of course, other family members. In all likelihood, a mountain of paperwork would also be encountered along the way to help determine eligibility for a variety of programs and services.

In other words, there's nothing routine about assisting aging parents. It is an ongoing and time-consuming process that requires careful thought and dedicated responsibility.

My wife, for example, takes her mother to numerous doctor appointments, helps keep her medications organized and makes sure her household is functioning in good order. In a similar manner, I have a retired brother who quarterbacks my parents' calendar.

Aging is so much more than getting older. There are not only financial and health issues; there are personal and logistical issues as well. A lot of time and money is spent on health related programs.

Along with many others in the financial services industry, I work to help retirees achieve financial independence. But that's just part of what needs to be done. Family members and other support groups need to step in and assist aging parents in the non-financial aspects of life. That's becoming increasingly difficult in this mobile world where family members live and work across the entire globe.

It was the late Art Linkletter who said, "Old age isn't for sissies." But, as moms and dads age, I tip my hat to those that take time out of their schedules to help them. The retirement years are much more than health and finances. They are also about sons and daughters stepping up to assist with things that money just can't buy.

The world is indeed complex. Senior homes today are filled with technology to help keep parents safe in the event of an issue. A case in point is my mother, who set her building fire alarm off early one morning when she burnt her toast a bit.

A minor incident, yes, but the safety alarms were there just in case. And it's with an appreciative smile that I look back today and say thank goodness for the technology.

———∞———

Ken Morris
As seen in Oakland Press 7/21/13

Own your home, don't let your home own you.

It's nice to see the housing market finally perking up. For a while, I forgot the many sights and sounds associated with home construction. It's actually quite nice to see and hear them once again.

Now that it seems we've turned the corner, I'll never again complain about the noise of hammers banging at sunrise. I know there are quite a few readers out there looking to trade homes or build this summer.

I don't ever want to hear about someone losing their home because they made a poor financial decision. I want to make sure potential homebuyers are armed with all the necessary knowledge as they search for that perfect house. Home buying, after all, is an investment. And, as with any investment, it's essential to keep your emotions in check.

So, before anyone considers the purchase any home, there are a couple of financial issues that I'd like to bring to your attention.

Most of you are undoubtedly aware of the first issue, the recent increase in the mortgage interest rates. Although there is no direct link, mortgage interest rates do seem to move in the same direction as the U.S. 10-Year Treasury bond yield.

In June of 2012, the 10-year yield was hovering near 1.5 percent. Just one year later, right after the recent July 4th holiday, the 10-year yield was 2.65 percent, 73.3 percent higher than it had been.

During the same one-year period, depending upon the terms of the mortgage, rates moved from the 3 percent range to more than 4 percent. That's a smaller increase percentage wise, but still one-third higher. However you want to look at it, the bottom line is that it costs more to borrow money now that it did one year ago.

The second area of concern is that it appears our elected officials will change the rules regarding the deductibility of mortgage interest. I obviously can't say for sure what the new rules will be, but when politicians start talking about changing the mortgage interest deduction rules, it's a good bet that the taxpayer will be paying more.

This past April, Michigan's Dave Camp who is Chairman of the House Ways and Means Committee, held hearings to discuss the elimination of income tax loopholes. Shortly into the hearings, changing the deductibility of mortgage loan interest moved from the back burner to the front burner as something that should be changed.

This followed a similar recommendation by the Simpson-Bowles commission study, which sought ways to lower the nation's deficit. In fact, one of their plans called for the elimination of all credits and deductions and reducing personal tax brackets to just three, 8, 14 and 23%.

And not to be outdone, President Obama has also proposed ending the mortgage interest deduction for all tax filers who are above the 28 percent income tax bracket.

Naturally, it is anybody's guess what changes will ultimately take place. But there definitely appears to be sentiment to make changes. The important thing then, when buying a house, is to not factor in the tax benefit of mortgage loan interest. It will likely change and perhaps even disappear in the next few years.

So please, when buying a home purchase one you can own rather than one that owns you.

Ken Morris
As seen in Oakland Press 10/6/13

Politicians must make tough fiscal decisions like the rest of us.

Politicians have once again seized the headlines. It's not because of anything they've accomplished, but rather what they have failed to do time and time again. Listening to our elected officials is like having a bad dream that just won't go away.

For many years as a financial advisor, I have assisted a large number of households with their budgeting and spending. Families are used to making difficult financial decisions.

To make their budgets work, I've advised households to improve their cash flow by doing such simple things as increasing the deductible on their car insurance or refinancing their mortgage to a lower interest rate. Sometimes, even changing their cable carrier was meaningful.

For other households, there were more complex issues. For example, income tax planning and distributions, charitable donations were part of the equation in establishing a budget.

In other words, as an advisor I've helped people resolve their budgeting issues with solutions that ranged from easy to complex. But even though there's a solution for most situations, you first have to acknowledge that a cash flow issue exists. Only then can the problem be resolved. And that's something households across this nation do each and every day

Sadly, our elected officials have chosen not to face financial reality. There have been many warnings signs, including the much-publicized Simpson-Bowles Commission, which pointed out in great detail that our nation is on an unsustainable financial path.

The commission even offered solutions. But it appears that many politicians are far more focused on winning the next election than on working to solving our national debt crisis.

In the near future, we will get the September 30th fiscal year-end numbers for 2013. Unfortunately, I don't expect good news. According to the Treasury Department, through August 31st, the first eleven months of this fiscal year, tax revenues were $2.473 trillion. Outlays were $3.228 trillion.

So the shortfall is a mere $755 billion. In simple financial terms, that means our nation brought in 77 cents in tax revenue and borrowed 23 cents for every $1.00 it had to pay out.

As a financial advisor, can you imagine my discussion with a husband and wife who spent their money in this manner? In all likelihood, a household that spent like this would be on the path towards bankruptcy. And I'd probably be referring them to a credit-counselling agency.

But our nation just doesn't work that way. Even worse, politicians are reluctant to admit that a problem even exists.

Again, according to the Treasury Department, in mid-September of 2007, the national debt was a staggering $9.01 trillion. In the last six years, another $7.73 trillion have been added to the debt. We're now an incomprehensible $16.74 trillion in debt. And it grows every day.

The politicians point fingers at one another; each political party blaming the other for fiscal woes that threaten a government shut down. Households across the nation have clawed their way out of financial crises. Businesses have regrouped, retooled and reinvented themselves.

But problems and issues cannot be resolved unless they're addressed. There's a spending problem in our nation's capital that should have been addressed years ago. All we ask of politicians is to make tough fiscal decisions like the rest of us make each and every day.

Ken Morris
As seen in Oakland Press 2/2/14

Finding a job isn't what it used to be.

A few days ago, a couple of my grandchildren were visiting. They know that I'm in the financial services profession and that I write a column. When I asked them if there was a particular topic they wanted me to write about, one suggested Zambonis and the other said garbage trucks. Don't worry, neither has a place in a personal finance column, but it reminded me that, years ago, my firm hosted the late Art Linkletter at one of our retirement education seminars.

In the early days of television, long before HD, Mr. Linkletter had a show with a feature called "Kids say the darnedest things." He was also one of our nation's first retiree advocates, and famous for the quote, "Old age is not for sissies."

Connecting the dots between the innocence of youth and retirement are the many years of being in the workforce. For many, working is a task or a chore, done for a paycheck. For others, like me, it's not so much work as it is a passion or career.

In other words, work is more than just a paycheck. If you look beyond the news reports that show unemployment numbers going down, you'd find that there are a staggering amount of Americans who would rather be in the workforce than wringing their hands and giving up.

As parents and grandparents, we have to do our very best to prepare our families for a world that will be far more complex than we could ever imagine. When Art Linkletter first aired, there were only a few stations. Television pictures were fuzzy and in black and white. One can only imagine what TV technology will bring into our homes in the years ahead.

I recently came across a study published by bankrate.com which indicated that people would not only move out of state to take a job, but also that four of ten young adults factor in health care benefits in the job selection process.

I mention this because there's an image of 30-year-olds living in the basement, dependent on the Bank of Mom and Dad. Uncle Sam is about to spend millions encouraging youth to sign up for health insurance coverage. I'm a bit baffled because the bankrate.com study already shows that health care coverage is important to young adults.

What doesn't get written about often enough are the young adults who boldly leave the comfort of home for their jobs rather than live in the basement. Most of the young adults I know are driven and have no desire to remain dependent on their parents.

For example, my youngest son graduated from college in a very tight job market. He left the comforts of home to find work in Texas. He soon found it, and worked around the clock for a low wage doing some of the dirtiest jobs in the Texas oil fields.

It paid off. In just over a year, his talent and work ethic were recognized and now, just a few years later, he has climbed the corporate ladder. He's doing so well, he can now afford to fly mom and dad in for a visit. I would like to tell my youngest son, the Texan, how proud I am and wish him a Happy Birthday.

Ken Morris
As seen in Oakland Press 3/8/15

Preparing for the inevitable.

For the second time in nine months, I buried an aging parent. This time it was my mother-in-law. On one hand, my wife and I were very fortunate to have them for as long as we did. But, as so many others have, we learned that assisting aging parents requires a lot of love, patience and time.

Unfortunately, aging parents often spend a lot of time at medical facilities. That being said, my hat's off to the professionals in the health care industry. It was quite gratifying to see a doctor stop by the funeral home and comforting for my wife to receive condolences from other doctors.

It was my first real experience with hospice workers and I was truly impressed with the professionalism and the heartfelt concern they displayed.

As children, our parents make our decisions. As they age, we become their decision makers. That's why it's so important to know what they really want when they're no longer capable of deciding for themselves.

As a financial advisor, I can't stress enough the importance of planning for inevitable events. No matter how difficult discussions may be they can lead to appropriate actions and help minimize potential family conflict.

To my dismay, many go entire lifetimes without drafting a will or trust. Even approaching the back nine of life, they fail to complete the Durable Power of Attorney forms for health care decisions.

Ignoring discussions doesn't eliminate problems; it often makes them worse because there is no resolution. It's unfair to put too much on one sibling's shoulders without adequate instructions or documentation.

Even when planning for life goals such as retirement, it's important to prepare for the unexpected. You never know what lies ahead. I've worked with numerous clients that never quite close the planning loop.

For example, many have accumulated a substantial nest egg. When asked if all their children are capable of handling a large lump sum distribution, most couples smile and point out that one of their children will quickly and inevitably blow their inheritance.

With proper planning, you can put restrictions for specified beneficiaries on IRA distributions. With trusts, you can also dictate periodic distributions as opposed to lump sum.

A frequent mistake I encounter is aging parents putting their financial assets into joint ownership with adult children. Even if they all get along, how do the assets get distributed fairly to others without gift tax or adverse income tax issues? In most instances, they cannot.

Without proper life planning, families can be torn apart over money issues while mom or dad is hospitalized. The time to do end-of-life planning is when you're in good health and have your wits. All parents should dictate what measures they want taken by medical professionals.

My father's wishes were clear and there was no need for the emergency medical teams to attempt revival. My mother-in-law's wishes and instructions made it easier for my wife and her siblings to say enough is enough and bring her home one last time.

Proper financial planning isn't just accumulating wealth for such life goals as a college education. It also includes end-of-life instructions and post-life distributions to loved ones and charities, thereby enabling happy memories to live on. Poor planning can often lead to family turmoil and conflict.

———◦◦◦———

Ken Morris
As seen in Oakland Press 5/17/15

May your launch be successful.

This is the time of year when many of life's transitions are launched. There are a lot of young adults graduating from high school who will soon be leaving home for the very first time. Similarly, there are lot of young men and women who are graduating from college, ready to step out into the world and hoping to become self sufficient.

In a perfect world, all of them would either be launching their professional careers or continuing their education in a specialized program such as medical or law school.

But the world isn't perfect. Yes, the economy may be improving, but far too many young adults will be returning home to mom and dad, still seeking their destiny.

May is also what I refer to as the beginning of the wedding season. In fact, it was exactly one year ago that one of my sons got married. And whether or not the bride and groom have matriculated through college, they too, are making a major transition.

So, we have high school grads, college grads and newlyweds, each of them embarking on lifelong journeys and all beginning in and around the month of May.

To all those young men and women graduating from high school or college or beginning their lives together with a significant other,

I offer a tip of my hat -- and some advice.

At many graduation ceremonies the speaker encourages the graduates to change the world in a positive manner. I agree that this is a wonderful and compelling message, but I offer something more specific. I want to encourage all young adults to be fiscally responsible.

What exactly do I mean by fiscally responsible? First and foremost, keep your debt under control. If you borrowed money to get through college, simply pay it back.

Unfortunately there has never been more college debt than there is today, but loans should be repaid. You can always rationalize why repaying your debt should be put on the back burner. But, at the end of the day, your debt is your responsibility, not your fellow taxpayers.

Another piece of advice is simply to live within your means. In this world you can quickly run up sizeable debt with a visit to Amazon and a few clicks. I'm not suggesting that you don't spend, but, just as with investments, balance is the key.

Finally, develop good savings habits. Don't just save what's left over, but rather become a disciplined saver. For example, start saving $50 per month and stick with it no matter what. A year later, increase the amount to $100. This is just an example, but making savings a habit is important.

I include newlyweds in the 'major transition' equation because, in financial terms, marriage is somewhat of a financial merger. You might be marrying into a large college debt or marrying someone who can't save a nickel.

Unfortunately, money disagreements are often cited as a reason why marriages don't succeed. My suggestion is talk about money prior to tying the knot. Both parties should be aware of the circumstances.

I believe it's important to develop proper money skills and habits. Over the years, I've observed that those who have a grasp of their finances turn out to be more responsible, generous and confident in their future.

Ken Morris
As seen in Oakland Press 3/13/16

Can you spare $20 for a cup of coffee?

Earlier this month I was blessed with my fourth grandchild. Amazing because I'm so young. Well, young at heart, anyway. Shortly thereafter, I was talking to my ten-year-old granddaughter who is pretty good at math.

I explained to her that she, her younger brother and new cousin all have a legitimate chance to see the year 2100. Naturally, she was amused at the thought that she would someday be old like grandma and grandpa.

Then I told her that my grandpa, with whom I shared a bedroom for many years, was born in 1886. She was astonished that I was old enough to know someone who actually lived in the 1800s.

I bring this up in a financial column because, like aging, inflation is a slow process. You may not notice anything different hour by hour or day by day, but eventually you look in the mirror and don't recognize the startled person staring back.

Inflation is like life's wingspan. At one tip of the wing you can look back at what it cost your grandparents to live. At the other end, you can look forward and project how much your grandchildren will have to spend.

The Consumer Price Index is a great measuring stick of inflation. While the CPI didn't exist when my grandfather was born, it started about the time my ancestors entered the USA in 1913.

Using the CPI as a guide, a person today would need $24 to purchase the equivalent of $1 in 1913. The inflation rate from inception of the index through 2015 has averaged 3.175 percent per year.

Of course, nobody knows what the future will hold. But, lets project that 3.175 percent inflation rate through the year 2100. Mathematically, it tells us our grandkids would need 335 dollars in their pockets to buy what 24 dollars buys today.

You don't have to be mathematically inclined to realize the likelihood that the dollar figures will continue to get larger in the years ahead. It's not a pleasant realization. Especially since larger numbers don't necessarily mean that people in the future will be wealthier.

One of the geniuses of our world, Albert Einstein, extolled the virtues of compound interest. If we want to help our young ones jumpstart their finances there are many ways to help.

Those of you over the age of 70 could consider taking your mandatory IRA distributions and opening an investment for your grandchild. A 529 College Savings Plan is a good way to start. There are also some sophisticated estate planning options including gifting and life insurance.

In all probability the future will require a great deal of money. Nobody knows how our grandkids will be spending their money, but I can assure you the dollar amount will be staggering.

My grandpa probably paid about a dime for a cup of coffee.

Today a cup can cost anywhere from a dollar to five dollars. Imagine a world where a cup of coffee costs twenty dollars. Unrealistic? Maybe. But that's what our grandkids will likely see.

The world has certainly changed since my grandfather arrived at Ellis Island. I can't say with certainty what the world will look like in 2100. But I'm firmly convinced that things are going to cost a lot of money.

Ken Morris
As seen in Oakland Press 12/11/16

Your Uncle Sam is not setting a good example.

As a financial advisor, I'm always encouraging people to save and invest for their future. Paying for an education, buying a home and building a nest egg for retirement all require a great deal of money. And saving for these endeavors requires plenty of discipline. Spending, on the other hand, seems to come very easy.

Setting a little aside each and every payday can go a long way toward achieving long-term financial objectives. Frequent readers know that I continually emphasize the importance of saving and investing.

So I thought I'd flip the coin and talk about spending instead. It's easy for me to simply suggest to clients and readers they should spend less. But you need to be receptive. A spend less mindset requires awareness and discipline.

A simple illustration of how saving a little can amount to a lot is the morning stop at a premium coffee shop many people enjoy. If it's just $2 more per day than a traditional coffee, you're spending an extra $10 per week. If you work 50 weeks per year, you'll save $500 a year by simply drinking traditional coffee over premium.

This is just one small example. I'm sure there are many more in your day-to-say routine.

After seeing the shopping frenzy that began on Thanksgiving and ran through cyber Monday, it became quite apparent that people want a real bargain. But, in reality, astute consumers can find bargains and ways to save at any time throughout the year.

My wife is a great example. She always knows who has a bargain or a coupon and when the deals expire. That doesn't mean she buys something every time she has a coupon for it. Rather, she is constantly aware of who needs what and what constitutes a good purchase price.

A methodical shopper that has a pulse on market prices over the course of a year spends significantly less than an impulse buyer. The term I like to use as an advisor is prudent. Spending is okay when it's needed and purchased at a reasonable price. That's being prudent.

Preaching good spending practices for households is somewhat difficult when our own nation's leaders set such a poor example. Years ago, retired Senator William Proxmire who was known for pointing out inefficient government spending, was a guest speaker at my firm.

For years he bestowed the Golden Fleece awards, exposing what he considered the wasteful sending of taxpayers' money. Among the highlights were a $57,000 expenditure for the study of the size of airline stewardesses and $84 million for the study of love.

In spite of Senator Proxmire's efforts, Uncle Sam continues to spend dollars like an impulsive, inefficient shopper. Current Oklahoma Senator James Lankford publishes the "Federal Fumbles" Government Waste Report. Released at the end of November, his latest report highlights 100 projects that waste a quarter of a trillion dollars in government spending.

When it comes to your household, if you spend like Uncle Sam your house will be filled with unneeded merchandise and your credit card debt will smother you.

If you think things through and spend prudently, you put yourself in a good position to save a few dollars and set aside a few dollars to help achieve some of your goals.

Ken Morris
As seen in Oakland Press 9/10/17

Seniors beware! Someone is after your nest egg.

Far too many siblings have issues after mom and dad pass away. More often than not, it revolves around money. The problem often begins years before when one of the siblings takes charge of handling the parents' finances.

It often starts as simply paying for routine bills, but eventually evolves into almost complete financial control. Frequently, the non-financial siblings are suspicious because they were never involved and have no grasp of the finances. On top of that is often the belief that there was a lot more money in mom and dad's nest egg than they were being told.

Most of us are aware that senior financial abuse is an issue simply because the elderly are vulnerable. A recent study funded by insurance giant Allianz revealed that 52 percent of financial abuse was perpetrated by family, friends or caregivers.

Financial abuse is defined as using an elder's money or assets for personal gain or contrary to the elder's needs, wishes or best interest.

That's alarming but it illustrates why it's so important to have one's financial affairs in order. That means under the guidance of a trusted family member or friend in whom you have complete confidence that they know how to handle money.

Managing mom and dad's money is one thing, but equally important is maintaining good communication with other family members. It can be very time consuming.

Anyone electing to have one of their children handle their finances must make certain the son or daughter knows all the financial details. Additionally, I suggest that the children not selected should be told why.

Setting expectations for reasonable accounting of the assets may also help minimize the potential for any future misunderstandings. In other words, parents should be proactive before departing this planet. For example, to help minimize the chances of a family squabble, show everyone a blueprint of your finances and what your ultimate goals may be.

While the sibling in charge may be dedicating time and effort carrying out mom and dad's plans, another sibling might see it as financial abuse. It happens often and it stems from lack of communication and understanding of the aging parents' financial circumstances. What's considered to be abuse by some is frequently nothing more than not knowing the parents' wishes.

Taking care of aging parents' finances is an extremely difficult, almost full-time job. It's virtually impossible to act on their behalf if there's even a suspicion of inappropriate financial behavior.

That being said, the reality is that scammers come at seniors from all directions with the intent of prying away some money. It may have begun as well intentioned assistance, but over time, initial good intentions can cross the line and wind up taking advantage of an elderly senior.

From a clergyman to a home repairman and everyone in between, the elderly with money are vulnerable. To minimize the odds of financial abuse, seniors need to get their legal affairs in order and establish Powers of Attorney.

Communicating one's wishes and desires to family members is essential. But, at the end of the day, it's the aging parents' money and there's only so much an advisor or loved one can do to help protect them from the unscrupulous. Sadly, it's a challenge that only escalates the older they get.

Ken Morris
As seen in Oakland Press 2/18/18

Is someone taking advantage of your parents?

Recently, in a two-day period, I ran into three buddies, each of whom shared similar stories about their father's failing health. We discussed whether or not elderly parents should stay alone in their own homes.

Since I've been in that situation with my parents, I shared my thoughts with them. I believe that, at some point, we stop being sons and daughters and instead become our parents' parents.

That means accepting responsibility, taking charge of the situation, and making difficult decisions about their welfare. And that includes keeping a watchful eye their finances.

In fact, at some point it may be necessary to take total control because, sometimes, elderly parents just aren't able to tend to their own health and wellbeing.

Fortunately, the vast majority of people in this world are honest, caring and honorable, and do their best, not just for their aging parents, but for all elderly.

But as people get older they're more vulnerable to the criminal element of our society. In the financial services industry, Elder Financial Abuse is a much-discussed topic.

As financial advisors, we do our best to help prevent anyone from taking advantage of our most vulnerable clients. For example, if there's an unusual withdrawal request, we can question the transaction prior to processing.

Painting with a broad brush, the elderly are often vulnerable and naive in regard to their money. Unfortunately, that makes it easier for the criminal element to pry some of that money away from them.

Regardless of age, we're all aware of the potential for identify theft. That's why everyone needs to keep their personal information close to the vest. I'm still amazed that some people actually carry their Social Security card in their wallet.

Unauthorized use of credit cards is another major problem. And I could go on and on about hackers and the financial fraud that's so prevalent today.

In an effort to help minimize potential financial abuse of the elderly, Medicare is actually going to change their identification cards over the next twelve months, beginning this April. Social Security numbers will no longer be listed on Medicare identification cards.

The change will be automatic and no action needs to be taken. But, I would not be surprised to see undesirables trying to turn this change into an opportunity.

For example, making a phone call, asking a senior for personal data including Social Security number so they can issue the senior a new card. Or perhaps, sending a bill requesting payment in order to get their new card.

In other words, open the door just an inch and bad things can happen. Even if you're able to get mom and dad into a safe living situation, they're still susceptible to contact via telephone and the Internet.

At some point in life, you may have to step in and make difficult decisions for your parents. It's important that you fully understand their finances so if you see anything unusual, like an uncharacteristic bank withdrawal, you can step in immediately.

Familiarity with their finances will also make you more prepared to step in and take control if and when their health no longer permits. As your parents age, it's important that you're prepared to take care of them not only physically, but also financially.

Ken Morris
As seen in the Oakland Press 3/31/19

The best education money can buy?

One of the largest expenses a family will incur is very likely the cost of a child's education. To assist families with this financial responsibility, many programs that encourage saving are available.

The most common are the 529 college savings programs, which were originally intended specifically for post-high school studies. The newly implemented tax law, however, now allows them to help cover the cost of education prior to the college years.

Simply stated, the student is referred to as the beneficiary of the account. Any loved ones can contribute into the account, and 529 contributions grow tax-free. If used for a qualified educational expense, the monies come out of the account tax-free as well.

Clearly, the new legislation offers families several incentives to save for education. Most often, a parent or grandparent is the responsible party for the account. Generally, there is a large menu of investment choices from which you can select.

It's important to do your due diligence and research prior to making a commitment, because, as with any investment, it could decrease in value. On the surface, 529 accounts appear straightforward, but there are several investment firms offering programs, thereby adding to the complexity.

The high school years go by in the blink of an eye. Before you know it, there are ACT tests and college applications. More often than not it's a stressful process, especially if you have your heart set on just one or two schools.

Rejection is painful and no parents like to see their child hurt. Parents can offer guidance and encouragement, cheer them on, or provide a shoulder to cry on. But at the end of the day, there is very little a parent can do to affect the outcome.

At least, that's what I thought. Then the recent headlines hit revealing the corruption of the college admission processes at what are considered elite universities.

Perhaps I'm naïve but I'm stunned at the magnitude of the corruption in college education admissions. The world is far from perfect, but pay-offs and bribes have no place in either the public or private sector.

I anticipate there will soon be more criminal charges. And don't be surprised if we soon hear that the IRS is taking a look at unreported income and financial transactions. I suspect this story will be in the news for some time to come.

I bring all this up in a financial column because I work day in and day out with families that want the best for their kids and grandkids. They save and invest, but they never cross the line called ethics. That's because they understand that achievements reached by cheating are hollow. And doors that are opened by money are likely to soon slam shut.

That being said, I'm a firm believer in networking. I'm frequently asked, "Who do you know?" or "What would you recommend?" Often as not, I suggest local chambers of commerce and civic organizations. They're great, legitimate places to meet people and open doors.

That's how relationships can be built and connections made that help beyond just the business world. What's unfolding before our eyes regarding college admissions is clearly wrong. In today's competitive world, education is important and expensive. But real education cannot be bought. It must be earned.

CHAPTER **3**

There's no crying in baseball or finance.

Ken Morris
As seen in the Oakland Press
3/2/08

What does the government do with your hard-earned tax dollars?

Today, I'd like to salute all those readers that are in the workforce, grinding it out every day. Even with an extra day in February, you've somehow, someway managed to make it through the month. Now we're entering a new month, and with it come new challenges. Every morning, you're off to work without a complaint because you're doing what you have to do to take care of all the responsibilities that go along with having a family.

March is a very meaningful month and it has the potential for a lot of distractions. There's the excitement of basketball's March Madness, the parties on St. Patrick's Day and for many, the most sacred time of the church calendar arrives in late March. The end of March is also the end of the first quarter. For many employees, that means extra hours at the office to make certain all the quarterly reports are in good order. So, between the hectic pace at work and the daily responsibilities of raising a family, there's very little time to just relax.

With so much going on, it's easy lose sight of the looming income tax deadline that is fast approaching. If you haven't gotten a handle on your taxes by the end of March, it's easy to enter April in panic mode. That's why I urge everyone to get his or her taxes completed accurately and on time. Take a long, hard look at the numbers and absorb them before filing them away.

So far this year, every employed person out there has been laboring away, not for the benefit of their family, not for the college educations or retirement nest eggs, but rather, for the benefit of the various levels of government. Last year the Tax Foundation, which has been around since 1937, proclaimed April 30 as Tax Freedom Day. That means the average American worker took until April 30, 2007 to cover their federal, state and local taxes. Your particular tax-free date may have been sooner or later, but so far this year, it's likely that all your efforts at work have not yet benefited you or your family. Not a very pleasant thought with that mid-April tax-filing deadline rapidly closing in.

Paying taxes is a fact of life in the United States. We may begrudge it a bit, but we all do it. And we certainly deserve to know that our hard-earned money is spent fairly and wisely. That's why it's vital for you to really analyze the numbers in your return. Don't be satisfied just because you got through it all in the nick of time and discovered that you don't owe anything additional.

Take a good look at what you send to Washington in both income taxes and Social Security taxes. Take a good look at what you pay in state and property taxes too. If you really delve into the numbers, you might not like what you see. But you should know these numbers and what they represent. Roughly one-third of your money goes to taxes in one form or another. Ask yourself if you're confident that the recipients of these tax dollars are good stewards of the money we entrust to them. Because there's a good possibility you won't be.

Ken Morris
As seen in the Oakland Press
4-12--09

Unlike basketball, investing rules change frequently.

It certainly was exciting having the NCAA Final Four basketball tournament in town, especially with Michigan State being on the big stage. One of the things I like about basketball is that, for the most part, the rules are consistent at all levels of the game. Another constant in basketball is the height of the rim. Every basketball fan knows that the rim is 10 feet from the floor, whether it's at a high school gym. a college field house, a professional arena or the playground down the block.

It seems improbable to compare basketball to investing, but that's exactly what I am going to do today. First let's lay a little groundwork utilizing the unmanaged Standard & Poor's 500 Index. As you are probably aware, this is one of the most frequently used measuring sticks for tracking the performance of the domestic stock market.

Last year, as was the case for many other indexes, the Standard & Poor's 500 was down 37 percent. Prior to last year, however, from 1926 through 2007, the average performance of the Standard & Poor's 500 was just over 10 percent per annum. While that number is accurate, it can nonetheless be misleading. That's where my little analogy to basketball comes in to play.

Getting back to basketball, can you imagine what it would be like for a three game series to be played with the rim at a different height each game? For the first game, the rim would be set at 5 feet. The next night, the game would be played with the rim set at 15 feet, and the final game with the rim set at the standard 10 feet.

Now, you could say that the average rim height was 10 feet, but obviously, all three games would have significantly different scores. Still you would be perfectly accurate if you said the scores were put up with the rims set at an average of 10 feet.

Okay, now let's get back to our market measuring stick, the un-managed S&P 500 Index. It's accurate to state that from 1926 to 2007, the average rate of return has been about 10 percent. But as with the height-changing basketball rim, in the 83-year history of the S&P 500 Index, there have only been 5 years in which the annual return was actually close to the 10 percent range. This information comes from the well-respected research firm Ibbotson Associates.

The reality is, like the basketball rim that keeps getting moved higher or lower, the actual annual *return* has very seldom been any-where near the actual *average*.

Imagine how difficult it would be to enjoy a basketball game with the rim at a different height every time. But the investment game is like that, with an up and down rim. It's unpredictable.

It's important to realize when investing, that the historical average seldom means much when establishing your goals for any particular year. If you're expecting a predictable return based on the average, you need to reset your expectations.

In reality, you can never quite be certain what to expect when you enter the financial arena. On the surface, average returns are a factor, but they can be misleading compared to actual year-by-year performance. Don't let a moving rim surprise you.

Ken Morris
As seen in The Oakland Press 7/29/12

Avoiding 'financial cliff' may require an Olympian effort.

After much anticipation, The Summer Olympics are finally underway in Great Britain. I have no doubt they will be exciting, and if history is any indication, we'll be seeing both heroics and heartbreak on our HD television screens.

It's a given that in sports there are both winners and losers, but the Olympics offer a different slant because we see athletes from remote parts of the world compete.

Somehow, it's more interesting and exciting that way. It's a special thrill to see athletes showcase their skills on an international stage and to follow the inevitable human interest stories that develop.

Those who have been paying attention to what's been happening around our state this summer have witnessed somewhat of mini British invasion. Michigan has hosted two senior professional golf tournaments, and both trophies are going across the pond to England. Meanwhile, the Henry Ford is displaying artifacts of the Titanic for the next few months. Coincidentally, I recently enjoyed a play about the Titanic at the Stagecrafters in Royal Oak. So, you may be wondering, just exactly what does all this have to do with a financial column?

If you've been watching or reading the financial news lately, you've undoubtedly encountered the term "financial cliff." That's precisely what our nation is rapidly approaching- a self-imposed financial cliff that's resulted in a fair amount of economic uncertainty. Hopefully, it won't culminate in an economic Titanic, but it could easily result in turbulent economic waters, if it hasn't already.

And, of course, we're all very well aware that this is an election year. To be honest, I'm already tired of political ads full of half-truths and misrepresentations. Truth be told, if it weren't for the Tigers, the

Summer Olympics and football, I would turn off the television until after the Olympics.

There has been a lot of fanfare about the uniforms of the U.S. Olympic team. Politicians have railed about the fact that they were not made in the USA. I cannot dispute that fact, but what truly upsets me is that many of the politicians who are so angry about the uniforms are the very ones leading us down a financial path without direction.

On numerous occasions I've brought to readers' attention that our nation has not had a budget in three years. Not to minimize the uniform fiasco, but I believe, in the big picture, the financial stability of our country if far more important than the uniforms our athletes wear.

Those leading the charge against the uniforms are the ones in charge of our nation's finances. And yet, they have not approved a national budget for three years in spite of the fact the law mandates it. Equally important is the fact we have income tax rates set to expire, a new 3.9 percent surtax and a 2 percent Social Security tax break about to end. These are real issues that need attention.

I can't imagine that, when the Titanic was slowly sinking, the captain's primary concern was the crew's uniforms. His efforts were to save the ship. I'm not suggesting our nation is going the way of the Titanic, but without question we have hit an economic iceberg.

Instead of worrying about the uniforms, our leaders should be working toward righting the economic ship.

Ken Morris
As seen in Oakland Press 3/16/14

The responsible way to keep tax records.

For many readers, this is another three-day holiday weekend. Tomorrow is a day that a lot of people will call in to work claiming they're ill and can't work on St. Patrick's Day. There will probably also be a spike in illness two weeks later when the Tigers open the season at home on Monday, March 31.

Although I'm not Irish, I can certainly understand the St. Patrick's Day festivities. And, who can't get excited about the Tigers? Even if you're not a baseball fan, the Tigers opening day is a sign that winter is over.

Personally, I save my "sick day" for April 15. Like many, I feel fortunate from a financial perspective. But, even though the government takes so much taxpayer money, what upsets me most is not the amount, but their poor stewardship of our tax dollars.

For as long as I can remember, every year there seems to be a number of public junkets on the taxpayer's dime. An IRS Star Wars party comes to mind. Plain and simple, Uncle Sam tends to be inefficient and wasteful when handling money. It's enough to make anyone ill.

In just a few weeks, I'll start receiving emails from clients asking how long they need to keep their tax records. My answer is a lot longer than many tax experts suggest.

Call me a pack rat, but I disagree with experts who claim you can get rid of your tax records from three to six years after filing. I can cite many examples where old returns, along with supporting data, have come in handy.

For example, Social Security no longer sends paper statements. You're responsible to log onto their website and review your records. Early in my career, I had some clients near retirement whose Social Security data showed they had $0 income for two years. My clients knew it was wrong, but it was their responsibility to prove the information was inaccurate.

What better way than an old W2 to substantiate your claim? Can you imagine having to postpone your retirement because records showed you didn't have the proper ten years in the system? Old tax records can also be used as your "proof of purchase" on an item you depreciated on your tax returns over a number of years.

Another situation I've often encountered with clients is confusion over whether or not their IRA plans are deductible. Old tax records can help an advisor or tax preparer reconstruct the records to help unwind the problem. After all, who wants to pay tax on the same dollar twice?

Over the years, I've also sat down with a surviving spouse who had little to do with handling family finances. Old returns can be an advisor's window into past investment activity. In fact, once while going through a widow's pile to shred, I discovered records that resulted in a sizeable amount of money for her benefit.

These are just a few examples of how old tax returns can be beneficial. It might not be as exciting as souvenir beer mugs from St. Paddy's Day or the Tigers' opening day program, but I suggest you also find room in your basement for your old tax returns and supporting data. You never know when it might pay off.

Ken Morris
As seen in Oakland Press 8/2/15

It's not easy to play by the rules.

Our nation loves winners. In 2012 our own Miguel Cabrera won the baseball triple crown. This summer, in horse racing, American Pharoah won the Triple Crown. The U.S. women's soccer team became world champions for the third time.

In golf, the young superstar Jordan Spieth was seeking the third leg of golf's Grand Slam. His putt to get into the playoffs missed by inches.

I bring this up because other than improvements in equipment, sports are essentially the same, year in and year out. The size of the baseball diamond hasn't changed over the years and the length of a soccer field has remained the same for as long as I can remember.

Golf embraces its storied history with the Grand Slam as thoroughbred racing does with the Triple Crown. I believe one of the reasons we enjoy sports so much is that we essentially know what to expect out of these events every year. And even though they're somewhat predictable, they're nevertheless entertaining and thrilling.

Unfortunately, virtually all aspects of life and the financial services industry are pretty much the opposite of sporting events. In life, although one can work hard by exercising and maintaining a good diet, there's no assurance of a lifetime of good health. When it comes to family issues, I've always maintained there are no Ozzie and Harriet households. At the end of the day, most families have faced challenging issues.

When it comes to investing, most readers understand by now that the majority of investments change value every business day. I have often stated that before an investment is made, three things need to feel right: Your mind, your heart and your pocketbook.

If something doesn't feel right, seek further clarification or don't make the investment. Also, before making an investment, I suggest making a mental commitment of staying with it for at least 36 months.

The bottom line is that investing is often unpredictable. And our nation's tax laws, combined with an overwhelming regulatory environment, make predicting even more unreliable. It seems the tax laws are tweaked and changed so often that it makes long-term tax planning close to impossible.

When I meet with colleagues from various professions, the primary and consistent complaint is the paperwork mandated by regulators. Life and money rules consistently change while sport rules remain pretty much constant.

When it comes to the economy, people often talk about the good old days when the economy was growing at a much faster pace than it has in recent years.

Experts all seem to have their opinion. And while there are a lot of factors, I think two reasons are the lack of clarity about taxes and an overabundance of regulation. The NFL training season is about to begin. Can you imagine taking any NFL lineman and putting him on the back of the horse? I can virtually guarantee you that the horse won't win.

In a sense, a heavyweight jockey riding a horse is analogous to our economy with all of the regulations riding its back. It seems to me that the economy performed much better when the rules were simple and predictable. Maybe our elected officials can learn something from our nation's love affair with sports and the champions and that have achieved extraordinary results.

Ken Morris
As seen in Oakland Press 11/1/15

The riskiest gamble you can take.

As a financial advisor I continually like to remind investors that there's no such thing as a sure thing. You can look to the past to see how an investment has performed, but as the cautionary disclaimer often warns, past performance is no guarantee of future results.

Over the years, we've heard many fallacies about sure things. In the investment world, some recent examples of certainty claims that didn't quite pan out are: real estate can only go up in value; day trading tech stocks will make you so much money you'll be able to buy your own private island; gold can only skyrocket in value; and most recently, oil can only increase in value.

At one time or another, most of us have seen commercials implying the above statements are fact. They are not. Just as it is with life in general, there are definitely no sure things in the world of investments.

Locally, we recently witnessed the near impossible. A couple of weeks ago Michigan State made an unbelievable comeback against Michigan in the last 10m seconds of the game. According to the statistical firm Massey-Peabody Analytics, the probability of Michigan

State winning the game was .02 percent.

Said another way, the likelihood of Michigan winning with only 10 seconds remaining was 99.98 percent. But whether you're a Wolverine or Spartan fan, you are now certainly aware that more than a 99 percent probability does not mean 100 percent certainty.

That being said, regular readers of this column know that I'm a strong proponent of using math and statistics to enhance your investment results.

Statistically, would you rather have a high probability for achieving your financial goals, or hope to reach those same goals by hoping for a statistically improbable event to occur?

The practice of making consistent contributions into your retirement plan is a good example of improving your probability for a successful retirement. For example, by saving $500 every pay period and taking advantage of compound interest, you can amass a sizeable retirement nest egg over a 30-year work career.

Statistically speaking, I'm pretty confident that the person in the example above will have a much, much larger retirement nest egg than someone that gambles $500 at the local casino every pay period for 30 years.

One of the things that concerns me is that far too many people are counting on a miracle win for a successful retirement. Don't be swayed by the Spartans near impossible victory. The actual statistics for anyone getting a financial windfall are nearly impossible to determine. And yet too many still reach for the highly improbable by purchasing lottery tickets or squandering paychecks at the casino.

In other words, gaming is well beyond entertainment for some. They're grasping for a nearly impossible result in order to achieve their retirement dreams.

What we all saw on the football field in Ann Arbor was about as improbable as you'll ever see in sports. True, there are no real guarantees in the world of investing either. But rather than hoping or gambling on the near impossible, it's wiser to put statistics in your favor.

It may not always work out as planned, but the alternative of counting on a near miracle is no way to achieve your financial dreams.

Ken Morris
As seen in Oakland Press 3/11/18

Think of retirement planning as an Olympic event.

The recent Winter Olympics were a nice break from all the squabbling among our politicians. But that diversion from reality was shattered when I heard about the high school shootings in Florida.

Watching the Olympics was enjoyable on many fronts. I found the ice-skating to be entertaining, the downhill skiing exhilarating and the curling almost addictive.

Athletes put their hearts and souls into their particular sport and the difference between a medal and going home empty handed is often a fraction of a second. Think about it; years and years of training and success or failure can be determined by as little as one-hundredth of a second.

There are many lessons that can be learned from the events over the past few weeks. Lessons about money and lessons about life.

To be successful in the financial world you need to have a goal. And, once established, you must stay committed to that goal.

The retirement programs offered at many places of employment are a good example. Let's say your goal is to save ten percent of your income annually, whether you have a 401(k), 403(b) or some other plan.

You need to stay true to that commitment! You shouldn't abandon your goal because you suddenly want money for other things. It might mean foregoing some hoped-for pleasure, or settling for a bit less than you wanted.

If it means putting off a vacation until next year, then put it off. If it means stopping at the coffee shop once or twice a week instead of every day, then cut back. In short, you need to display the discipline of an athlete. Yes, even an Olympic athlete.

My years of experience as a financial advisor tell me that saving is the most important component of a worry-free retirement. Even more important than investment selection.

Spending and saving are obviously connected, like the two ends of a seesaw. If one end is out of sync, things just don't work. For example, if a family claims they're saving twenty percent of their income, but have outrageous credit card debt, I'd say they're not saving as much as they claim.

An in-depth, behind-the-scenes look at athletes shows us their hard work and dedication and the sacrifices they make to achieve their goals.

Of course, your financial profile will never be on prime time television, but working with a financial advisor is like having a one-person prime time audience.

Over time, a financial advisor knows and understands how hard you've worked and how much you've sacrificed. It's sort of like having an Olympic coach. One that can teach you, help measure your progress, keep you on track and be a good listener and motivator.

Success just doesn't happen on its own, it takes a team.

The recent Florida school shootings are a reminder that life not only can change, but even end in a split second.

No matter what your goal or how much you plan and prepare, everything can change forever in the blink of an eye.

When I present a financial plan, I always remind people that I want to help them achieve their financial goals and objectives, and just as important, to enjoy life's journey with their family members.

Because we simply don't know what tomorrow will bring.

Ken Morris
As seen in Oakland Press 4/8/18

How many clubs are in your investment bag?

Since the market lows of just over ten years ago, in general the equity markets have essentially been appreciating steadily without any significant pullback. The appreciation hasn't always been consistent, but overall, the trajectory has been upward.

That is, until recently. We've now entered into what technicians refer to as a market correction. That's defined as a retreat of at least ten percent from the equity market's peak.

As an advisor for many years, I have frequently observed investors become bolder and bolder with personal investment strategies that I believe added unnecessary risk to their investment portfolios.

In sports, a baseball team can carry 25 players on its roster. Golfers can carry 14 clubs in their bag. Why would a team carry fewer than 25 players? Or a pro golfer fewer than 14 clubs?

Obviously, you want to carry the maximum allowable; it just makes sense. You never know when you might need a fresh pitcher because you're going into extra innings, or a particular golf club because you're under a tree.

The investment world can be very complex. As an advisor I always want to do the best I can for my clients, even if it means taking them down a path that might seem complex.

I would never want any investor to have only13 golf clubs available. I want them to have access to everything that's available, even if an additional investment might be a bit more difficult to explain and understand, or carry a slightly higher fee.

At the end of the day, I want all hands on deck for long-term investors, especially those clients that are risk averse. It's a matter of simple mathematics. If you had exactly $100,000 and suffered a 20 percent loss, your account value would stand at $80,000.

A common misconception is that you would only need to earn 20 percent back in order to break even. Not true. A 20 percent gain would bring you up to $96,000. You'd actually have to appreciate by 25 percent to get back to even.

Suppose you were supplementing your income by withdrawing 4 percent from your investments every year. With a falling market, you'd only be compounding the problem because the account is already decreasing.

The combination of a falling account value combined with making withdrawals to supplement your income could be devastating. Many investors prefer to use a portion of their nest egg to generate reliable, predictable income regardless of overall market performance.

Just because an investment is complex in nature, it doesn't mean it's bad. What is bad is if you find your nest egg depleted years from now because you didn't have a segment of your portfolio allocated to an asset class that offered you steady, reliable income because your advisor thought the asset class was too complex to explain or understand.

Every investment isn't for everyone. We all have a different mental makeup and different grasp of finances. I firmly believe it's important to listen to each client's concerns and to make every resource available to help them resolve their concerns.

By excluding a particular asset class, an advisor could put you in a situation where you have to go a lifetime without considering an investment that could be beneficial to you down the road.

CHAPTER **4**

How times change.
Beam me up, Scotty,

Ken Morris
As seen in The Oakland Press 6/6/11

Real labels thoroughly, spend judiciously when it comes to grocery shopping.

Recently there were a number of news stories about a man who ate his 25,000th Big Mac. The national newscast that I saw was the typical of the interviews you see when somebody does something unusual.

High on the list of questions asked were several inquiring about his health. Surprisingly, to me at least, he was in extremely good health.

Following the interview, the news station immediately brought in their medical expert, who was amazed that this Big Mac lover was not only in satisfactory health, his cholesterol level was just fine.

As you might expect, the medical expert considered this circumstance an anomaly and strongly recommended that viewers not maintain their diet in a similar fashion.

While the focus of the story was clearly one of nutrition and health, I was at amazed that nobody in the news media ever brought up the financial aspect.

By my calculations, this gentleman spent a small fortune at MacDonald's. Assuming he spent $5 for each burger, with its attendant soft drinks and fries, he has spent in the neighborhood of $125,000 on Big Macs. And that got me to thinking about an issue we all face; spending money on food.

In today's world, people are much more health conscious than generations past. I'm a good example in that I exercise regularly, and on most days, try to eat healthier.

I realized recently that I could no longer run into a grocery store and just pick up an item. Let's take peanut butter, for example. In days past, I would see two peanut butter brands I recognized, and then make the big decision between crunchy or smooth. On store shelves today, there are far more brands and many more choices than just crunchy and smooth.

I have also become a conscientious label reader and often find them confusing. On some labels, there is such an array of information that I sometimes believe the intent is to confuse.

Monounsaturated? Polyunsaturated? Hydrogenated? Partially hydrogenated? And that's the easy stuff. I almost feel like I should bring a nutritionist or maybe even a chemist with me to help sort through the ingredients.

Some labels even emphasize things that are not in the ingredients. And then there's the organic question. How many items have that word on the label? I have to ask myself, should everything be organic? Aren't there some safe chemicals that can help fruits and vegetables grow without jeopardizing out health?

While doing my research on organic, I've found various and sometimes even conflicting definitions of the term, which, of course, adds even more confusion to my shopping.

Finally, being a grocery store label reader, I have become aware of the term Fair Trade Certified. In a nutshell, this means that in the process of bringing in foreign food such as coffee, the foreign workers are paid fairly and have satisfactory working conditions.

All this information brings havoc to the food budget. I believe that the cheapest food price might not necessarily be the healthiest food choice.

The ultimate result is that, as the world becomes more complex, it requires more financial decisions. And when it comes to health, I urge you to read labels thoroughly and spend judiciously, keeping in mind that the cheapest is necessarily the best.

Ken Morris
As seen in Oakland Press 4/27/14

Personal observations on a high-tech world.

In the late 1970s, just before we were married, my wife and I purchased our first home. At that point in my life, I didn't have a lot of household items to bring to the marriage. In fact, I didn't even own a single piece of furniture.

To the best of my recollection, my entire contribution to the new home all fit into my small car. One trip across town was all I needed to move. You could say the house was vintage. It had a built-in milk chute and a large, gas-gravity furnace that used to burn coal. With its large, octopus-like arms reaching out in all directions, it dominated the basement.

Upstairs, the thermostat was very simplistic. If you wanted more heat, you turned the knob to the right; if you wanted less, you turned it to the left. Our television had a rabbit-ear antenna for controlling the reception and we changed channels manually, not remotely. The VCR? Well, we were still saving to buy one.

As our family grew, so did the houses and the technology within them. Today, with all the boys grown up and on their own, we decided to move again. With just the two of us, it just made sense to get smaller and simpler. Well, the new place is definitely smaller, but I'd hardly call it simpler.

I remember when telephones were just for talking. Today, they're essentially mini computers. I'm still amazed that I can control the volume on my television with my phone. And instead of having speakers and audio equipment around the house, we have a remarkable device called a sound bar. It not only provides incredible sound on the television, it can also play all the music on my wife's phone.

Our high-efficiency furnace takes up only a small portion of the basement compared to the old octopus. My new thermostat looks like something from NASA. It tells the outdoor temperature, the indoor temperature and humidity and even gives a seven-day forecast. And, of course, I can control it with my phone.

Throughout my lifetime, technological advances have amazed me. To an extent, they've also confused me. That's why I had "technicians" tutor me on how to use the television, sound system and thermostat. Yes, it was a little embarrassing to have to contact a technician in order to adjust the household humidity.

Now, when I buy a new computer or software program, I educate myself. In today's high-tech world, almost everyone needs some sort of help or self-education to understand these incredible new products. I believe the days of just selling a product like a television without tech service and ongoing education are numbered. People are making careers out of servicing high-tech equipment and educating the users.

The world is certainly more complex, but the benefits are well worth the time to learn how to operate a television, furnace or, for that matter, any other household item.

It's easy to overlook how fast technology is changing our personal lives. I noticed how it improved things at the office and in the financial world. But my recent move really made me aware how much it has changed our day-to-day living at home. We've come a long way from milkman delivery and newspapers on the porch.

Ken Morris
As seen in Oakland Press 2/15/15

Is anything "Made in America" anymore?

There's absolutely no question that we're competing in a global world. Not that many years ago, when my sons were away at college, I informed them that they would be entering and competing in an environment where a nation's boundaries would be blurred from a business perspective.

Fast forward to today, just a few years after my sons graduated. The line between domestic companies and foreign firms is even more blurred than it was when I told my sons what to expect.

For example, right here in our own backyard, Chrysler uses the advertising slogan "Imported from Detroit." And yet, Chrysler isn't exactly in our backyard. Their parent firm, of course is Fabbrica Italiana Automobili Torino (FIAT), which, as the name implies, is in Turin, Italy.

Right down the street, General Motors manufactures and markets vehicles all over the globe. And now, for the very first time, Ford is selling the iconic Mustang overseas.

The point is that it's extremely difficult to be just an American firm that markets only to Americans. Most people are aware that this phenomenon goes well beyond the automotive industry. Many other American firms, like McDonald's and KFC, market their products over the entire globe.

But it's vital to keep in mind that we are not alone. Other companies throughout the world also understand that boundaries are blurry. They, too, market and manufacture their products throughout the world.

Just as many American manufacturing firms have plants overseas, many foreign-based automotive firms have manufacturing plants in the U.S. And the components they use might have been designed or manufactured anywhere.

The "manufacturing team" may have had engineers from multiple countries working on a product to be sold throughout the world. In today's tech world, the reality is not nation competing against nation, but rather company competing against company.

I may be somewhat old school, but being a Michigander my entire life, I try to support our local car companies. I understand that they likely use parts and components made overseas. But at the end of the day, it makes me feel better when I have a car in my driveway with a local nameplate on it.

I'm aware that it's not always the best decision to purchase a product just because it's manufactured locally. But when I'm shopping for something, a tie always goes to the local company.

One of the nicest Christmas presents I received was a Shinola watch. I recently had the good fortune of touring their manufacturing facility in Detroit. I was really impressed with the dedication of the employees. I saw hard work, commitment, enthusiasm and pride.

Yes, all the components might not have been made domestically, and maybe a competitor might have a watch that keeps just as good time for less money. But I like the feeling of being able to see some of the faces of workers who put some effort into a product I use.

Even though we're a "global" manufacturing world, I still like to see if I can help some of the local hands involved in global efforts.

Investors can invest with their conscience, perhaps choosing to avoid alcohol and tobacco companies. Likewise, as consumers, we can be both smart and thoughtful on how we spend our hard earned dollars.

Ken Morris
As seen in Oakland Press 3/15/15

Traveling back through time and into the future.

Some popular old television shows seem to live on forever. Seinfeld comes to mind, but I believe one television show in particular has gone where no other show has gone before. I'm speaking, of course, about Star Trek.

Leonard Nimoy, aka Dr. Spock, recently passed away. You might forget that he was a stage actor, an author, a poet, a film director and a photographer. You might forget that he had recurring roles on other television series, including Mission Impossible and Fringe.

But you will never forget that he was Spock.

The Spock character he played as an actor was probably his greatest life defining moment. No matter what he did after the Star Trek television series, he was always typecast as Dr. Spock. Years later, even though he was much older, the producers found ways to incorporate his character into the Star Trek film franchise. He even directed a few of them.

Yes, Star Trek and Dr. Spock bring back many memories of the sixties. But Star Trek was a television show, not real life. Many other significant cultural and social events were taking place. Many other people were rising into prominence.

In no particular order, when I think about the sixties, I am reminded of the Kennedys, Dr. Martin Luther King, the Beatles and the British Music Invasion, the Ford Mustang, social unrest in Detroit and, of course, the Tigers winning the 1968 World Series.

I do not mean to slight anyone here. Certainly there were many more significant events and great accomplishments. These people and events are simply those that quickly came to mind.

Getting back to Star Trek, it's been almost 50 years since it first aired in 1966. At that time, there were no 401(k) retirement programs.

In fact, the deductible IRA didn't come into existence until 1974. True, life expectancy was less than what it is today, but at that time you just had Social Security and savings.

Some, especially autoworkers, were fortunate enough to have pensions, but for most other hard-working citizens there were no other retirement accounts.

A common method for measuring the cost of living is the Consumer Price Index. Using the CPI inflation calculator, it would take $7,200 today to be the equivalent of $1,000 in 1966. I mention this because I fear that too many retirees seem to ignore that costs tend to go up over time.

But while costs may increase, technology improves and competition helps keep costs down. I doubt any of my readers or clients are watching the same television set they had in 1966. Since Star Trek debuted, we now have microwave ovens, wireless telephones, computers, E Readers and Dick Tracy Watches.

The calculator I paid plenty for in college can now be bought at the supermarket for a few dollars. And yet, the cost of living will probably continue to increase over time. Perhaps at an astronomical rate. That's why people need to continue saving and investing.

As long as research and innovation continue, the quality of life is likely to improve. And with it, the cost of living. Nonetheless, I'm hoping that someday soon, instead of going through the hassles of the airport check-in, I will simply be able to ask the airline attendant to beam me up.

Ken Morris
As seen in Oakland Press 3/13/16

Can you spare $20 for a cup of coffee?

Earlier this month I was blessed with my fourth grandchild. Amazing because I'm so young. Well, young at heart, anyway. Shortly thereafter, I was talking to my ten-year-old granddaughter who is pretty good at math.

I explained to her that she, her younger brother and new cousin all have a legitimate chance to see the year 2100. Naturally, she was amused at the thought that she would someday be old like grandma and grandpa.

Then I told her that my grandpa, with whom I shared a bedroom for many years, was born in 1886. She was astonished that I was old enough to know someone who actually lived in the 1800s.

I bring this up in a financial column because, like aging, inflation is a slow process. You may not notice anything different hour by hour or day by day, but eventually you look in the mirror and don't recognize the startled person staring back.

Inflation is like life's wingspan. At one tip of the wing you can look back at what it cost your grandparents to live. At the other end, you can look forward and project how much your grandchildren will have to spend.

The Consumer Price Index is a great measuring stick of inflation. While the CPI didn't exist when my grandfather was born, it started about the time my ancestors entered the USA in 1913.

Using the CPI as a guide, a person today would need $24 to purchase the equivalent of $1 in 1913. The inflation rate from inception of the index through 2015 has averaged 3.175 percent per year.

Of course, nobody knows what the future will hold. But, lets project that 3.175 percent inflation rate through the year 2100. Mathematically, it tells us our grandkids would need 335 dollars in their pockets to buy what 24 dollars buys today.

You don't have to be mathematically inclined to realize the likelihood that the dollar figures will continue to get larger in the years ahead. It's not a pleasant realization. Especially since larger numbers don't necessarily mean that people in the future will be wealthier.

One of the geniuses of our world, Albert Einstein, extolled the virtues of compound interest. If we want to help our young ones jump-start their finances there are many ways to help.

Those of you over the age of 70 could consider taking your mandatory IRA distributions and opening an investment for your grandchild. A 529 College Savings Plan is a good way to start. There are also some sophisticated estate planning options including gifting and life insurance.

In all probability the future will require a great deal of money. Nobody knows how our grandkids will be spending their money, but I can assure you the dollar amount will be staggering.

My grandpa probably paid about a dime for a cup of coffee.

Today a cup can cost anywhere from a dollar to five dollars. Imagine a world where a cup of coffee costs twenty dollars. Unrealistic? Maybe. But that's what our grandkids will likely see.

The world has certainly changed since my grandfather arrived at Ellis Island. I can't say with certainty what the world will look like in 2100. But I'm firmly convinced that things are going to cost a lot of money.

Ken Morris
As seen in Oakland Press 2/26/17

Get those old records off the shelf...

My wife recently saw Beautiful, a play about the life of the iconic Carol King whose record Tapestry is one of the best selling albums of all time. The play sparked her interest and she is currently reading the history of many female musicians of the early 1970s.

Since I'm a better financial advisor than a shopper, I thought I'd be on to something good if I could find music from other female artists of the 1970s era.

Fortunately for me, vinyl records are making a comeback. I recall that in my high school days record albums were $1.99. Many thought vinyl records would become obsolete with the advent of the 8-track player. Not so.

In retrospect, it was funny that the tape would occasionally rewind in the middle of a song. Same for those tiny cassettes; so small they fit into your shirt pocket. They had issues, and almost anyone who owned cassettes can remember rewinding them with a pencil.

From there we went to CDs, then the technology boom came and today you can carry an entire music collection in your cell phone.

But for my taste and apparently many others agree, music is best when played on vinyl. Proof? Records stores are reviving throughout the area.

In fact, many well-known stores are now selling new albums. Locally, Shinola, which made its name in quality wristwatches, now manufactures and sells turntables.

Technology may be nice, but there's nothing like putting a record on a turntable, blowing the dust off a diamond needle and enjoying your favorite music.

As a financial advisor, I was curious what that album I paid $1.99 for in 1970 would cost today. Using the Consume Price Index as a measuring stick, I calculated that $12 today has the purchasing power of $2 in 1970. I must note, however, that most of the new record albums I see today cost in excess of $12. In fact, many are in the range of $17 to $25.

I bring this up because most of us have a financial reference point in our lives from which we measure current prices. I believe that reference point is established when you begin paying for items with your own money as opposed to mom and dad's.

It might have been a first new car that cost less than $10,000. More likely, it was a candy bar or package of gum, that cost 5 cents or a bottle of coke from a vending machine for a dime.

On the surface, a record album that costs $15 sounds outrageous, especially with a reference point of $2. Because one end of my financial measuring tape is the 1970s, spending $40,000 for a vehicle or having a $2,000 per month house payment also sounds outrageous.

As an advisor, I occasionally see retirees go without, because in their mind what they're looking for costs too much. But, if they did the math they might discover that the purchase price really didn't increase significantly. Rather, inflation dictated that more dollars were needed.

More often than not, when we reflect on the past, we tend to look back with fondness. Many thought vinyl records were a thing of the past, but today, this "old technology" is preferred by many, including this financial advisor.

Ken Morris
As seen in Oakland Press 10/28/18

A tale of inflation, stagnation and innovation

The iconic Sears Roebuck & Company, known these days simply as Sears, announced two weeks ago that it was filing for bankruptcy. Another rock-solid American company has lost its way.

As recently as the late 1990s, Sears was one of the coveted Dow Jones Industrial 30 stocks. Many experts described Sears as the pre-Internet Amazon of its day. With its famous catalog, mail order business and brick and mortar stores that anchored many malls, Sears was once a dominant retailer. It just couldn't keep up with consumers.

As a financial advisor, I often used a 1976 Sears Catalog to help educate clients. It displayed a woman's wool and mohair fleece coat for just $79.50. Children's solid color high-top Converse sneakers were only $12.70. And you could put a spiffy new set of radial tires on your car for $37.00 apiece.

As you've likely surmised, I did this to illustrate the impact of inflation. When looking through the catalog, people would get a chuckle out of the low prices, not to mention the clothing styles of the day. And for many, it also brought back fond memories.

One tool for measuring inflation is the Consumer Price Index inflation calculator. Using it, those $12.70 Converse high-tops would cost about $55.00 today. And those $37 tires would be $162.00.

I bring up inflation because it's something you need to factor into your financial planning. While nobody knows how much prices on goods and services will increase, it would be naïve to believe they'll remain stable.

Proper planning must anticipate rising costs. For the 90,000 Sears workers and retirees, the Pension Benefit Guaranty Corporation immediately issued a press release to ease their concerns. The PBGC has been working with Sears for several years, and although the pension is underfunded by a whopping $1.5 billion, it predicted it would be able to deliver earned benefits the vast majority.

Many people aren't aware that the PBGC was established during President Ford's administration. It's a federal agency funded by insurance premiums paid by healthy private sector pension funds.

There are roughly 40 million people covered by private sector pensions. About 1.5 million are receiving their failed pension benefits through the PBGC.

The Sears bankruptcy is another example of the difficulty of staying on top in corporate America. Sears had a fantastic run, but somewhere along the way mistakes were made. They did not adapt to changing times.

The employees and retirees of Sears are fortunate for the existence of the PBGC. But the rise in PBGC premiums is one of the reasons so many healthy corporations discontinued their pensions in the first place.

Without doubt, the retail world is extremely competitive. In its heyday, the Sears catalog was a great way for consumers to see what was new and exciting. The brick and mortar Sears had a department for almost every need. But technology has changed things. People shop much differently today.

Another American icon may have fallen, but in a strange way that's what makes America great. In the business world, you can't afford to be complacent. Somebody is always trying to build a better, cheaper mousetrap.

With competition there are winners and losers. For decades Sears was a winner. But it's virtually impossible for an aging giant to survive among the Amazons.

CHAPTER 5

Where's the crystal ball.

Ken Morris
As seen in the Oakland Press
4-6-08

It's time to face the reality:
You can't count on Social Security.

As the April tax deadline rapidly approaches, people need to be aware that not everyone who earns an income is required to pay income tax. Our federal income tax code is structured so that low wage earners do not have any federal income tax liability. That being said, all wage earners, regardless of tax bracket, do have money withheld from their paychecks for Social Security and Medicare.

For Social Security, the first $102,000 of one's wages is subject to a 12.4 percent payroll tax. There is no such income cap for Medicare, and everyone has 2.9 percent withheld from all of his or her income. With both Social Security and Medicare, the employee and employer share the tax equally. Those who are self-employed, of course, must bear the entire burden themselves

Every year, the trustees of these programs provide a report that spells out the financial situation of the programs. This year, as in years past, Treasury Secretary Paulsen, who recently spoke at the Economic Club of Detroit, had nothing but gloomy news.

The bottom line is that the problems facing these two programs cannot be ignored. It can no longer be said that the status quo should be maintained because it has worked in the past. Change is an absolute necessity. The financial issues must be addressed. If they continue to be ignored, it is a virtual certainty that they will ultimately reach a point where they cannot be repaired.

Some very important and difficult decisions need to be addressed before both these programs are on life support. Indeed, they may already be. That isn't a politically popular notion, but unfortunately, sometimes the truth is unpleasant.

According to the recent report, Medicare's hospital insurance program will begin running a cash deficit later this year. The annual study also projected later this decade that Social Security will begin sending out more than it takes in. Without question, the amount that's being spent on these programs is a large slice of the federal budget pie. Without significant changes, it will only get larger

What will it take to reverse these financial deficits? First, because the trustees of Medicare issued a funding warning, our next president, whoever he or she may be, is required to submit a reform plan. This was mandated by a provision when the prescription drug program was added to Medicare in 2003. The trustees have warned that the cash influx needed to keep Medicare functional will require a significant increase in withholding over the current 2.9 percent of all income.

The Social Security side doesn't look any brighter. The trustees estimate that it would require either an 18 percent cut in benefits or an increase of withholding from the current level of 12.4 percent to nearly 15 percent.

The problems these programs are facing should not be sugar coated. The reality of the situation is that both programs cannot continue to function the way they are today without making some significant changes.

I am hopeful that our elected officials do not play politics with these programs. The problems are real and the solutions will be difficult. To ignore them is unconscionable, as it would burden our children and grandchildren with a financial anchor that they simply do not deserve.

Ken Morris
As seen in The Oakland Press 5/9/10

Do homework before cracking into nest egg.

It's no secret that an inordinate number of people in this area have retired in the past few years; many of them not by choice. Regardless of the circumstances, as any individual enters his or her retirement years, there are several important financial issues they need to address.

When to begin drawing Social Security benefits is an important and often difficult decision to make. Determining when and how much to withdraw from your retirement nest egg is equally important. That's what I want to focus on today. How much can you afford to withdraw from your nest egg each and every year?

First, let me emphasize that it's extremely important for your money to last as long as you do. That's obviously difficult to gauge, because nobody knows when they'll meet their maker. In general, though, people are living ten to twelve years longer than they were just 60 years ago.

In other words you should plan on having a monthly income for at least 120 months longer than retirees in the 1950's.

When to start taking money from your nest egg depends on your individual financial circumstances. IRS rules dictate that you must begin withdrawing by April 1 of the year following the year you reach 70 ½. At that time you are obligated to take a required minimum distribution as determined by an IRS life expectancy table. But let's assume you're one of the majority of people who can't wait that long. How do you provide for reliable and predictable income for a lifetime?

Many financial advisors have access to insurance driven income programs with formulas to help determine how much and when to withdraw. But they're full of disclosures and disclaimers that are too long to address in this limited space.

Fortunately for hands-on investors, there's another way, utilizing a simple mathematical formula. I believe it's a relatively safe approach, but it isn't guaranteed and it does requires some attention at least once a year.

The formula is simply a 4 percent annual withdrawal. Using this strategy makes it unlikely you'll ever run out of money, although you will see fluctuations in annual income.

Suppose you had $100,000 at year's end. A 4 percent withdrawal would give you $4,000 of income, leaving $96,000 in principal. Now suppose you did well the following year and your investment grew from $96,000 to $110,000.

A 4 percent withdrawal would then boost your income to $4,400. That's great, but let's say the markets fall and your principal drops to $90,000. More bad news is that your 4 percent withdrawal now amounts to just $3,600. Clearly, your income varies from year to year using this strategy, but the likelihood of running out of money is minimized.

While this is just one of numerous strategies you can utilize, it's a good place to start because you can measure and refine it as you go. I worry about retirees who just wing it and hope for the best. Hope is not a strategy.

So, if you plan to tackle the retirement income issue on your own, you should at least consider the 4 percent withdrawal strategy. On the other hand, with something as important as lifetime income, it might be wise to review your situation with a qualified financial advisor.

Ken Morris
As seen in The Oakland Press 6/20/10

Putting money where you think it's safe isn't always the case.

For years, I've been helping individuals in the automotive industry tackle their various retirement offers. Sometimes, the would-be retiree had plenty of time to contemplate, digest and analyze the details of the package that was offered. On other occasions, it was just a matter of a couple of days before a decision was needed.

Fast-forward a few years to the present. Today, it's the dedicated people in our educational systems that are faced with retirement offers. The incentives to retire vary slightly by district, but overall, the pensions are pretty much carved in stone. It's simply a matter of determining which survivor pension benefit best suits the needs of the individual's family.

But there is a difference between the state's retirement program and those offered by the various automotive companies. The difference is the consequence of turning down the offer. Simply stated, if an educator turns down the retirement offer, it's possible that their ultimate pension could be less than the currently proposed numbers. Future contracts might also bring about a smaller pension.

The stark reality is that, after 25 to 40 years of service in education, many educators are at the finish line. Supposedly, these early retirements are going to help ease some of Michigan's financial woes.

But, I see the situation differently. I see an enormous amount of talent, similar to that in the automotive industry, that will be out of work come fall.

In both the private and public sector, it appears that an era has ended. There are no more congratulations and gold watches after a career of dedicated service. For many Michiganders, the end of their career came rather suddenly.

I believe the decline in defined benefit pensions signal the end of an era. Defined benefit pension plans are not usually associated with lump sum dollar amounts. A defined benefit plan statement, for example, wouldn't say you have $250,000 in your retirement account, Rather, the benefit would be stated as a monthly pension amount, say $3,000 per month.

Unfortunately, workers from both corporate America and the public sector are seeing pension programs being frozen or terminated. So future retirees will not have the financial security that many of their counterparts enjoy today.

What does it all mean? Come fall, our schools will be lacking a lot of experienced educators. This should serve as a wake-up call for everyone. In the future, financial security won't come from years of service in either the public or private sector. It will have to be the result of prudent financial planning and disciplined investing by the individual, regardless of occupation.

I recently came across data from the mammoth mutual fund company Fidelity, which handles several 401(k) programs. The average 401(k) account with Fidelity is less than $70,000. I realize we're in the midst of a difficult investment environment, but people need to step it up and increase their savings.

Let's suppose a 401(k) is worth $100,000. An aggressive withdrawal rate of 5 percent would generate just $5,000 of annual income, and it would be taxable.

That's a far cry from the $2000 to $3000 per month pensions that many retirees currently enjoy. Times are different. It doesn't matter whether you work in the private or public sector. Now is the time to prepare for a world without pensions.

Ken Morris
As seen in The Oakland Press 5/20/12

Lump sums for retirees:
Do the math before you get the payout.

I've mentioned on many occasions that pension plans known as defined benefit plans are becoming dinosaurs. With the economy unable to gain traction and the corporate world tightening its belt, one of the most logical places for a company to cut costs is within its retirement plan.

Getting rid of the traditional pension plan can save any business a bundle of cash. In our local automobile industry, if there is a pension plan for active employees, it's been frozen and replaced with a 401(k) program.

So, in essence, veteran employees and current retirees are the only ones who will benefit from traditional pension plans. But even this scenario appears to be changing.

Ford recently announced it would contact existing retirees and offer them a lump sum buyout. Rumors are that others will follow. From Ford's point of view, I can certainly understand why they would like to minimize this huge future liability.

From a retiree's standpoint, however, I see very few situations where this could be advantageous over the long term.

Years ago, President Reagan signed into law a bill sponsored by the late Geraldine Ferrara that impacted the pension plan landscape.

No longer could an employee take the largest pension plan payout without a notarized signature from his or her spouse. The largest pension payout ended at the death of the employee and left nothing for the surviving spouse.

While the Ferrara bill provided a slightly smaller pension payout to the employee, it paid a reduced benefit for the survivor's lifetime. In other words, most retirees who are now receiving benefits have some sort of survivor pension payout.

Structured settlements are another example where lump sum payments may be offered. Such settlements are the result of accidents or injuries, often involving litigation. You may have heard commercials for financial firms offering individuals a lump sum payment in lieu of the structured settlement.

But since structured settlements are often lifetime payments, taking a lump sum is probably not the best idea. I've rarely seen a structured settlement that made mathematical sense for giving up a lifetime income stream.

That's why I'm somewhat skeptical of the upcoming lump sum buyout option for those receiving a pension. It will be interesting to see what the lump sum buyout offers are. But I doubt the numbers will look better over a lifetime for retirees and their surviving spouses. That's not to say there won't be a few situations where it might be worth taking a hard look at the numbers. Pension payouts do end at the death of the second spouse. Typically, you can't hand off pension benefits to anyone but a surviving spouse.

So, if there's no surviving spouse and there is a desire to leave monies to surviving heirs, a lump sum might make sense.

For example, financially comfortable retirees might elect to roll their pension into a lump sum IRA Rollover and name a beneficiary. Whether it's a family member or a trust, it could result in a significant benefit where there otherwise would have been nothing.

As a financial advisor, I've learned never to assume. Although I am somewhat skeptical of lump sums, if given the opportunity, you should still take time to crunch the numbers and look at various "what if" scenarios.

Ken Morris
As seen in The Oakland Press 6/17/12

GM pension decisions force families to think hard.

I'm afraid the notion of a stress-free retirement without any financial concerns is a thing of the past. The days of gold watches and lifetime pensions and health care will soon be distant memories.

After many auto executives retired, they saw several changes in what they thought were benefits for life. Health care packages were trimmed, a great deal of life insurance was lost and many pensions were reduced. The GM bankruptcy process changed many lives.

Now, thousands of retirees from both Ford and GM are faced with a decision regarding their pensions. GM executives must decide by July 20. Yet another unanticipated item to deal with in what was supposed to be a stress-free time of life.

GM executives can choose to do nothing and simply continue to receive a direct deposit every month. After seeing the actual numbers, however, it's a far more complex matter. That's why I encourage careful analysis of the issue rather than defaulting to the convenient solution.

Each family faced with a choice must thoroughly look at all the financial options that relate to their own circumstances. When considering forgoing monthly pension checks, extreme caution is warranted.

I'm always skeptical when looking at traditional pension alternatives. Auto executives have the option of taking a lump-sum distribution into an IRA rollover instead of a traditional pension. But the proposed dollar amount of the lump sums varies from executive to executive, as do their individual circumstances. So there is simply no one-size-fits-all answer to the pension versus lump sum choice.

To some degree, the historical trade off between "spending it all in retirement" and "leaving it the kids" comes into play. If you choose to maintain your pension as is, it terminates at the death of the surviving spouse. There's nothing to pass on to the children, grandchildren or a charitable cause.

A properly managed IRA rollover, on the other hand, has the potential to be passed on to heirs and charities at death. Quite possibly, a multi-generational family fortune could even be built.

I believe the ability to pass on a substantial dollar amount to your heirs is one of the compelling reasons to select an IRA rollover over a pension.

Of course, there are other factors, like marital status and health. People who are single or in poor health might be better served by a lump- sum distribution into an IRA. Because, whatever the circumstances, you're in control with an IRA.

Without question, there's comfort in receiving a pension. But on the downside, there's never a chance of a pay raise throughout the retirement years. That's a real concern as life expectancies have increased significantly.

A pension, after all, is like a pay freeze. You're looking at the long road ahead without ever having a chance for a pay raise. You might become one of those retirees complaining about being on a fixed income. With an IRA rollover, there's a chance your income could increase in retirement. Of course, the potential for growth also brings investment risk.

The bottom line is that there's no clear-cut answer. You simply have to take time and effort to think it through.

If you would like details on educational classes that can help you sort through the numbers, please contact my office.

Ken Morris
As seen in The Oakland Press 7/1/12

The positive side of the lump sum vs. monthly check issue.

The Pension Protection Act of 2006 flew under the radar of most people, including a majority of financial advisors. It was not exactly front-page news. In fact, I would be shocked if it made the headlines anywhere other than in a few financial magazines dedicated to pension administration.

The primary purpose of the PPA was to strengthen and secure the funding levels of pensions. The ultimate objective was to protect the pension benefits of retirees throughout the nation.

As it turned out, provisions within the PPA opened the door for retirees to opt for a lump sum distribution rather than continue receiving the monthly checks of a traditional pension.

At the risk of trying to sound like an actuary, one key provision in the PPA permitted lump sum basis calculations to utilize investment grade corporate bonds instead of the 30-year U.S. Treasury rate in order to determine the lump sum values.

In the real world, where most of us live, this means little, if anything, to our daily lives. But in the world of funding pensions, this little noticed provision in the PPA, which was intended to strengthen pensions, actually enabled corporations to offer their retirees the option of a lump sum distribution in lieu of a monthly pension check.

So here we are today, getting ready to celebrate the 4th of July with barbecues and family get-togethers all over the country. My guess is that, in addition to discussions about baseball, politics and family members, there will be quite a bit of talk about the decision that so many retirees will soon have to make.

"Should I continue taking my pension or would I be better off taking the lump sum?"

While there's no one-size-fits-all answer to that question, there's absolutely no question that the financial world as we've known it is rapidly changing.

I've mentioned many times that traditional pensions are becoming dinosaurs. The lump sump buyouts of pensions will simply hasten their extinction.

There are certainly plenty of instances where continuing with a monthly pension check is the best choice. Just as there are other situations where a lump sum can lead to greater financial opportunities.

No matter which decision a retiree makes, as a financial advisor, I have seen many positives come out of all the discussions that are taking place. People are finally talking about money management and all that accompanies it.

I'm seeing that people are beginning to grasp the concept that that fixed income means no future increases in monthly checks. And it's likely that financial terms such as inflation and buying will make their way around the horseshoe pit on the 4th.

It's a positive thing that people are becoming more and more familiar with financial terms that tend to go with lump sums, like market risk and diversification.

It seems the pension issue has forced many families to actually look at their finances in a manner in which they probably never had to in times past.

I realize that many will continue to agonize over their decision right through the July 4th holiday. So it's crucial to look at the big picture. Having to choose between an income stream and lump sum is difficult. But it sure beats having no job, no income and no retirement nest egg.

Ken Morris
As seen in The Oakland Press 7/15/12

The possibility of living too long has become a financial fear

In the early 1980s, when I was a young pup in the financial services industry, the primary concern for most households was fear that the primary wage earner would die too soon. I don't want to dismiss the importance of proper life insurance planning, but it appears the thought of dying too soon has been replaced by the possibility of living too long.

Even today, I have new clients come into the office with a musty 25-year-old life insurance policy with a whopping face value of $5,000. Not to be critical of a $5,000 policy, but realistically, that amount of money is only going to sustain a surviving family member for a very short period of time.

These relatively small life insurance policies really illustrate how inflation can erode buying power over time. And in all likelihood, I believe we'll continue to see the cost of living increase in the years ahead.

I've always encouraged everyone to start saving and investing as early as possible. Setting aside specific investments and tax ramifications for a moment, and just looking at saving from a mathematical perspective, it's clear that it pays to invest early.

For example, a 30 year old who saves $100 a month at 7 percent until age 60 will have twice as much money at age 60 as someone who saves the same amount and gets the same interest, but delays starting until age 38. That's a significant difference.

A recent survey sponsored by Bankers Life and Casualty posed the following question to retirees: "What financial advice would you give to younger people about retirement?" A whopping 93 percent responded that they should start saving as early as possible.

Another survey question asked the retirees what aspect of retirement they would have liked to know more about. Again, the response was overwhelming. They wished they had known how to "make their money last."

This further illustrates that, as our population changes, living too long has replaced the fear of dying too soon as a concern of retirees.

A more immediate concern on the local front is the looming July 20 deadline for GM retirees. They're faced with the choice of taking and investing a lump sum or receiving a steady income stream from a group annuity.

Initially skeptical, I have been pleasantly surprised at the size of the lump sum offer from GM. Those that saved and invested through-out their working years have put themselves in a position where they can look at their entire portfolio and consider taking the lump sum.

If the lump sum is invested properly, the benefit is the opportunity to keep up with rising prices in the years ahead. On the other hand, those retirees who don't already have a nest egg should probably stay with the group annuity and hope their buying power won't be eroded by rising prices in the future.

There is no one size fits all solution, and everyone's circumstances are different. But one common thread for all retirees, not just GM, is that life expectancies are on the rise. It's a fact that people are living longer and a near certainty that the cost of living will continue to rise.

Thus, the great challenge for retirees today is to make their money last as long as they do.

Ken Morris
As seen in Oakland Press 3/9/14

The only person you can count on for retirement.

As we close in on the April 15 tax deadline, I want to remind my readers that it's not too late to consider making a contribution into an Individual Retirement Account (IRA) for tax year 2013. Without going into great detail, IRAs come in three flavors. There are the traditional tax-deductible IRA, the Roth IRA and the non-deductible IRA, each with its own unique features and benefits.

Determining which one you're eligible for and which suits you best can take some time. With the tax clock ticking, I suggest you move quickly to get everything completed by the tax deadline.

Now more than ever, it's extremely important to save for your retirement. If you believe you'll be fine in retirement because of your pension and Social Security benefits, you may want to reconsider. I've said many times that we're in a YOYO (you're on your own) world, and recent events make it very apparent.

For example, we hear about the Detroit pensioners on an almost daily basis. Former policemen, firefighters and other city employees are likely to see their pension checks reduced by as much as thirty percent.

Nobody knows what the final number will be, but it's sad to see any retiree take a hit to his or her pension check. Over promises, fiscal mismanagement, criminal convictions and increased longevity have all contributed to the crisis.

That being said, the problem is not unique to Detroit. It may be one of the first cities to deal with the pension crisis, but I receive

E-mails from an organization that tracks pension problems throughout the country virtually every day.

There's a laundry list of cities that aren't very far behind Detroit. It even appears likely that some states will be unable to meet their pension promises. Because of all the broken promises, real people are going to feel the pain of smaller pension checks.

In addition to the pension shortfalls that are sweeping the nation, the military recently announced cutbacks that will impact our military families' budgets. Details will soon come out, but it looks like we will again be witness to another broken promise.

Pension cuts and military cutbacks aren't all that concern me. If you're still working, take a look at your report on the Social Security website. It clearly states that, on its current course, there will not be enough to pay promised benefits in their entirety.

Unfortunately, it appears that we're entering an era of broken promises. My purpose is not to point fingers or lay blame. There's plenty to go around. I only want to motivate readers to save for retirement. It's really important because, at the end of the day, you shouldn't rely on your employers' promises to pay you after you retire.

Your retirement years shouldn't be full of stress, especially if you thought you had everything in good order. Unfortunately, that's no longer the case. I cannot fix the broken promises, but I can encourage everyone still working to save more on their own. If you depend some other source to finance your retirement, it just may not be there when you need it.

I'll say it again: You're on your own. So please, take control now. You can't afford to rely on others for your financial wellbeing.

Ken Morris
As seen in Oakland Press 9/28/14

The recession made your kids better financial managers.

I always enjoy reading surveys and studies that touch on American pocketbook issues. I recently came across the 2014 Planning and Progress study by the Northwestern Mutual Life Insurance Company. I found it to be quite an eye opener and I'd like to share my thoughts on some of their findings.

As a bit of groundwork, keep in mind that the worst economic meltdown our nation has endured since the Great Depression was just a few years ago.

That downturn caused many to lose their job or retire early. It also affected their kids, who got a first-hand look at what mom and dad were going through.

In a strange way, they benefited by witnessing their parents' financial struggles. According to the survey, their generation is a bit better at managing their finances than those aged 40 to 59.

In other words, those under 40 and over 59 are fairly disciplined in the way they handle their finances. Which means, according to the survey, those aged 40 to 59 are having a somewhat difficult time defining their financial goals and developing a plan to achieve them.

As a financial advisor, I can understand how this could happen. When times got tough and people were either let go or retired early, they had little choice but to put in extra long hours at the job, often doing the work that three or four others used to do.

What's more, while they burned the midnight oil and carried all that stress, their work benefits were probably scaled back. They likely saw their health care premiums increase and their pension plan disappear. While they were carrying the ball, the team became smaller and they were forced to do more with less.

For many in this age group, it was difficult to think about long-term planning at a time when they were working around the clock, fighting for financial survival.

This leads to one of my concerns as pointed out in the survey. For many, the solution to achieving a successful retirement is to remain in the workforce longer. That's easier now than during the recession, when it was nearly impossible for someone 60 or older to find immediate work following a job loss or early retirement.

Now, just a few years later, quite a few people plan to stay longer at their current job, with the intent of having more money when they ultimately retire.

That's an admirable goal if you actually enjoy your work and your health permits you to continue working.

I think it would be more prudent to plan for retirement between 62 and 65, then keep working longer, viewing the money earned beyond those years as somewhat of a bonus.

It appears the younger generation was paying attention during the downturn because they get it. They are well on their way to being the most financially disciplined generation in a long time and that's a good thing.

Generally speaking, it's the 40 to 59 year olds that need to shore up their household finances. But regardless of age or circumstances, I encourage everyone to take time to establish their financial goals and set reasonable steps to achieve them. Don't put yourself in a position where you have to work until you drop.

Ken Morris
As seen in Oakland Press 10/12/14

What if you're never President of the United States?

Slightly less than two weeks ago, former President Jimmy Carter turned 90. It's been thirty-three years since he left the Oval office. I am not saying that he's the oldest former president, but no other president has survived that many years beyond his term in office.

In a similar fashion, former President George H. Bush has also been living an active life since his term in office. I bring this up in a financial column because both former presidents illustrate the point that, for a variety of reasons, people today are living longer lives.

In fact, lifespans today are so much longer than in decades past, retirement can easily represent a third of a person's life.

Unlike you and me, neither of the former presidents has to worry about running out of money in retirement. Of course, their pension checks are funded by your tax dollars.

But longevity is one of the reasons that so many pension funds are either struggling or have been discontinued. Who could ever have imagined that so many people would live such long and fruitful lives?

By contrast, Civil War General and former President Ulysses S. Grant didn't have it quite so well as former presidents have it today.

—⚬✕⚬—

Ken Morris
As seen in Oakland Press 8/30/15

The give and take of Social Security.

In case you missed it, the nation's Social Security system program turned 80 on August 14. It was controversial when President Roosevelt launched the program and it remains hotly debated to this day.

One extreme compares the program to a Madoff type Ponzi scheme while the other end of the spectrum believes it's not only a great public program but also that its benefits should be expanded. In other words, even after eighty years the Social Security controversy remains unsettled.

Yes, I have concerns about Social Security, essentially because of the underlying mathematics. People are living much longer today and roughly 10,000 people retire every day. That means there are going to be a tremendous number of benefit checks going out even as wages remain somewhat stagnant for those still working.

Meanwhile, active workers today receive a statement that informs them there will only be enough money to pay 77 percent of projected benefits. Is it any wonder so many younger people have doubts about the program?

A recent AARP poll shows that 73 percent of people doubt Social Security will be able to pay promised benefits. So, while the big picture of the program continues to be debated, I have two comments about the program that seldom make the headlines.

One concern is that many people overlook the fact that up to 85 percent of their Social Security benefits are subject to income taxation when they're retired and receiving benefits.

He was elected to office at the young age of 46. When he
some poor financial decisions were made and he became
on his military pension.

Remember, there was no Social Security at the time.
der to supplement his retirement income and provide mo
heirs, he wrote his memoirs with the assistance of Mark Tv
passed away from cancer at the young age of 63.

In today's world there are definitely a lot more finar
for former presidents and other politicians after they have
Such financial security did not exist a hundred years ago,
days, I'm sure we would be shocked to hear that a former
was struggling with pocketbook issues.

My point is that the general public just doesn't have tl
income security that former presidents have. In fact, the n
people today are nowhere near being on the financial traje
would lead them to a worry-free retirement income.

As someone who works with a lot of retirees, my obser
been that most people who worry least about their retireme
are those that began preparing early in their careers.

Yes, they contributed regularly into an IRA or whate
retirement program that their employer provided. Just as i
they continued to participate in these programs whether the
ic times were good or bad.

Like former Presidents Carter and Bush, I would prefer i
one to have a relatively healthy and active retirement for m.
to come. Unfortunately, you won't have the financial benel
ing a former president. And, unlike President Grant, it's highl
ly you'll find anyone willing to pay you a bundle for your m

That's why it's incumbent upon you to make certain you c
age 90 with minimal financial concerns.

Having a reliable, steady income and a decent sized
doesn't just happen. It takes a lifetime of effort in order to r
retirement years the golden years we all dream about.

I find this to be quite bothersome. During your working years you're paying income tax on the money withheld from your paycheck that goes into Social Security. Then you're taxed again when you collect Social Security. That is double taxation, plain and simple. It wasn't always this way, but in an effort to strengthen the program the Greenspan commission suggested this provision and it was signed into law in 1983.

My other concern is the seldom-discussed fraud that Social Security attracts. We've all read about identity theft. It's a real issue in our society. In fact, a lot of sensitive personal information was recently stolen from the IRS coffers.

The Office of the Inspector General is finding out that identity theft is even a problem for the deceased. As a society, we generally celebrate the elderly, and rightfully so. The Gerentology Research Group recently concluded there were fewer than 50 people over the age of 112 worldwide.

Yet, from 2006 to 2012, nearly 67,000 people used a Social Security number for someone born before 1901. Clearly, criminals are using Social Security numbers of the deceased for fraudulent purposes.

Fraud is not just a problem for households and corporate America; it's also an issue for Uncle Sam and the Social Security program. The statistics prove it.

As the debate intensifies over how to strengthen the program, I hope improving the record keeping and monitoring cash outflow is part of the discussion. A more efficient program could result in more income for retirees or lower taxes for workers.

As a nation, we want our elderly to be able to live their lives with dignity. Although it's controversial, the Social Security program is part of the equation. But when life ends, Social Security numbers need to be permanently retired and kept from being used fraudulently.

Ken Morris
As seen in Oakland Press 2/28/16

Retirement is no longer a three-legged stool.

When preparing clients for retirement in the early years of my career, I would often introduce the concept of viewing retirement as a three-legged stool. The three legs were represented by the client's personal savings, his or her pension plan and, of course, Social Security. While all three legs were not necessarily the same size, all three were nonetheless vital sources of income during the retirement years.

But that was then, this is now. Things have changed over the years. Nowadays when preparing a family for retirement, it's very likely that the pension leg no longer exists. If by chance it does, the dollar amount of the benefit is probably not nearly as large as had been initially projected.

That's because many pensions were frozen several years ago and the pension benefit became fixed. The amount no longer increased with additional years of employment.

So today, the bottom line is simply that for people approaching retirement, the pension leg is either non-existent or very much shorter than anticipated early in their work careers. Unfortunately, for most young people beginning their career, there won't be a pension leg.

As our society moves away from traditional pension plans, more emphasis is obviously put on personal savings and Social Security. Any working person has a certain amount of control over how much they save. But they have no control over Social Security. And as I have expressed numerous times, I'm concerned about the financial strength of Social Security.

Like it or not, Social Security is deeply intertwined with politics. That's especially evident during an election year. I'm not necessarily criticizing the Social Security program as it stands today. I merely want to point out some of the red flags that are being waved by the Social Security trustees. Because it seems to me that the flags are flying under the radar.

I think it's great that Social Security statements are once again being sent to those in the workforce. I suspect that most people skim the verbiage and simply look at the tables that project their income at early, normal and delayed retirement.

I hope they're aware that the numbers are only projections, not promises. Because the statements point out that, on its current course, there eventually will only be enough Social Security funds to pay 77 percent of projected benefits. That's a legitimate concern that needs to be addressed.

I also want to bring to the attention of my young readers a recent error made by the Congressional Budget Office (CBO). An error they corrected in early February. Last fall, the CBO projections for people born in the 1960s and retiring at age 65 were incorrect.

It was initially projected that Social Security would replace 60 percent of income for middle income workers and 95 percent for those in the lower quintile. The projections were corrected to 41 percent for middle wage earners and 60 percent for the bottom quintile. That's substantially less.

I certainly understand that mistakes happen and commend that they were corrected promptly. But it doesn't change the big picture. The program needs attention sooner than later.

Before politicians talk about expanding the program, the very foundation needs attention. As it stands, the current program doesn't inspire long-term confidence. That makes long-term financial planning extremely difficult.

Ken Morris
As seen in Oakland Press 5/15/16

Who wrote your will?
Would you let a stranger write your will?

As a financial advisor I often communicate and work side by side with my clients' attorneys. More often than not, it's my insistent prodding that motivates them to get their legal affairs in order.

The reality is, not too many people like to talk about their mortality. For many, avoiding any discussions about wills and trusts means they don't have to endure that uncomfortable and difficult discussion with their spouse.

The recent death of the musician Prince has once again brought the subject of wills into the forefront of the news. I would like to emphasize that I am not an attorney, but I believe most of these news reports have it incorrect.

I'm referring to the contention that Prince died without a will. From my perspective, that's not exactly correct. Everybody has a will. If you don't write one for yourself, your state of residency already has one written for you. And you may not necessarily like it. In Prince's situation, the laws of Minnesota will be followed.

So it's safe to say that most of my readers have a will in the State of Michigan. Again, they either took the time and effort to write their own, or they must follow the guidelines of the will Michigan has drawn up for them. And it requires no signature, date or witness.

It's unlikely that many of my readers have an estate approaching the size of Prince's, but I still believe it's critical to take the time to get your legal affairs in order. I think it's preferable to pass the financial baton the way you want it, not the way Michigan has written it for you.

If you have a retirement account such as an IRA or 401(k), you must name a beneficiary. Just be sure to review and keep that information up to date. The same is true for your life insurance policies.

Investments that are held jointly automatically go to the survivor, but a word of caution. The surviving spouse could lose the tax benefits of the stepped-up basis. That's why I don't like it when a parent puts a child on an investment to make it easy at death.

Here are some points from the State of Michigan will for those who don't write their own. If you die without a spouse, children inherit everything. A spouse without children or parents gets everything.

In the case of a spouse and parents, but no children, the spouse inherits the first $150,00 of your intestate property plus 3/4 of the balance. Parents get the rest.

And for a spouse with descendants from either side, but no parents, the spouse inherits the first $150,000 of your intestate property plus1/2 of the balance. The rest is split among the descendants.

From my perspective as a financial advisor, everyone has a will. If you like the one written by the state of Michigan, which might entail the cost of a court appointed attorney, take no action.

But if you really care about your legacy and the unique circumstances of your loved ones, I encourage you to find an attorney in whom you're both comfortable and confident. I believe most people, with the assistance of a lawyer, can do better than what Michigan has waiting for you.

Ken Morris
As seen in Oakland Press 7/31/16

Beware. Your Uncle is smiling.

It's hard to believe, but every day in America 10,000 people reach the age of 70. For the next 18 years, the wave of baby boomers will be retiring and also approaching that important number. And nobody will be happier than Uncle Sam.

Why? Because at age 70½, retirees must begin taking withdrawals from their retirement accounts and paying income taxes on those distributions. And Uncle Sam is smiling because the first wave of retirees has arrived.

If you were born in 1946 between January 1 and June 30, this is the tax year to begin withdrawals. There's a loophole where you can wait until 2017, but then you'd have to take two taxable withdrawals in 2017.

These withdrawals are commonly referred to as required minimum distributions (RMDs). The IRS uses its life expectancy table to calculate the required amount, and for someone aged 71, that expectancy is 26.5 years.

Since most people don't like to spend their time reading government tables, I recommend a simple method to help people ballpark their distribution without getting too deep into the details.

First, you have to know the year-end values of your retirement accounts. Then you have to remember the number 4. Here's an example. Let's say the year-end value of your retirement accounts is exactly $100,000. Simply turn that 4 into a percentage, apply it to $100,000 and you come up with $4,000.

Yes, that's only a ballpark figure, but it gives you a pretty good idea of how much you'll need to withdraw without diving into all the specific details.

When you do get into the specifics you'll likely find that 4 percent is a bit on the high side, but at least it gives you an idea. I like to use this simple formula because I've found that most people have no idea what they're looking at when they hit the magical age of 70½.

The nitty-gritty details of reaching that milestone are fairly complex. For example, if you have both IRA and 401(k) retirement accounts, you can't take the total amount of your distribution from your IRA. You must take withdrawals from both accounts, even though the mathematical total is the same.

On the other hand, if you have multiple IRA accounts, you don't have to take a bit out of each one. You can take the total amount of your RMD out of any one of the accounts. As I noted, it's confusing.

But you absolutely must take the time to get it right.

I say this because the penalty for non-compliance is severe. How does 50% grab you? That's right, if your mandated distribution was $4,000 and you failed to make it, you'd be facing a $2,000 penalty.

So if you have IRA, 403(b) or 401(k) retirement accounts, you must take- and pay taxes on- distributions every year once you reach 70½. The distributions are added to your taxable income, which may put you into a slightly higher tax bracket. Another reason Uncle Sam is smiling.

I encourage everyone turning 70½ this year to meet with your advisor within the next few months. It's important that you get it right because the penalty for non-compliance is quite substantial. And the last thing you want to hear is Uncle Sam laughing out loud.

Ken Morris
As seen in Oakland Press 1/8/17

Is your pension a mathematically impossible promise?

From an investor's perspective, I'm looking forward to 2017. Naturally, nobody can predict the future. But with the dollar the strongest it's been relative to foreign currencies in more than a dozen years, I believe the stars are lined up to reward long-term investors.

That being said, investment rides are seldom smooth. Instead they tend to move more like a bumpy roller coaster. Although I'm optimistic for investors, there area few financial issues that we need to get a handle quickly. If not, I'm afraid the optimism will wane.

One of the potential powder kegs is something that affects almost everyone who works: pensions. The numbers behind pensions in America cause me great concern.

In simple terms, pensions are financial promises to deliver retirees a reliable, predictable check throughout their lifetime. Over the years, pensions have been negotiated with employees of municipal and state agencies, unions and corporations. Although it's difficult to lump them all together, they generally have one thing in common. They're in poor financial shape.

From coast to coast, there have been plenty of warning signs, which for the most part, have been ignored. Underfunded pensions are a teapot sitting on a hot stove. Eventually it will come to a boil. I believe the burner is getting hotter and wouldn't be surprised if 2017 is the year people across the nation will finally hear the warning whistle.

Chicago, New York and other cities have more retired police officers collecting pension checks than there are on patrol. In California, the Highway Patrol pension fund is near life support.

Residents of California will be seeing a ten dollar increase in their car registration fees to help cover the pension shortfall. Also in California, the pension fund manager Calpers is only sixty percent funded and has recently reduced their investment projections. Our neighbors in Illinois have similar underfunding problems.

On the local scene, the recent city of Detroit bankruptcy forced many retired city employees to take a haircut on their pensions. Throughout the country, many tradesmen whose pensions are through their union rather than their employer are anticipating a reduction in their pension checks. In other words, the promises are beginning to crumble throughout the country and I fear it's only going to get worse.

In Lansing, legislation was recently proposed that would have eliminated pensions for new teachers. It was quickly suppressed, however, because it was politically unpopular. Reducing or eliminating pensions, of course, is never going to be a popular political position. But the mathematics of underfunded pensions needs to be addressed. And the sooner, the better.

But the bottom line is that it doesn't matter whether or not you have a pension. You still must save and invest on your own. You just can't count on an underfunded promise, no matter who makes it.

Across the nation, too many promises have been made that are mathematically impossible to keep indefinitely. Many pension promises have already been broken and I fear many more will be in the future. At the end of the day, the math will always prevail. Two plus two will always equal four. *(Two dollars cannot pay a four-dollar obligation.)*

Nobody likes to see broken promises that result in retirees struggling with their finances. But in spite of pension concerns, I'm still optimistic for the long term.

Ken Morris
As seen in Oakland Press 8/13/17

The best place to retire is wherever you want to be.

I subscribe to numerous financial publications that touch on topics ranging from teaching children about money to hospice care for the elderly and everything in between. In short, about lifetime planning.

It seems like every article on retirement recommends, "The top ten places to retire." Most of them come with some sort of qualifier, like the place with the lowest taxes, the best weather, the best medical care or the best cultural environment.

Clearly, there are a multitude of quality retirement destinations, if that's what you're seeking. Based on the experience with my clients, however, most end up living relatively close to their children, at least at some point during their golden years.

There's no hard and fast rule regarding what you should do or when after retirement you should do it. In fact, many people are delaying retirement and working past the age of 65.

Many do so because they understand their nest egg isn't sufficient for today's long life expectancies. But a significant amount over the age of 65 continue to work simply because they enjoy it. It may only be part time or in an entirely different field, but they choose to work rather than riding off into the sunset.

I sense that a lot of people approaching retirement see these top ten places to live and feel almost obligated to move. But there's no need or rush to relocate. It's not something you have to do, even if you've given it a lot of thought.

For example, maybe you've been thinking about a particular area, perhaps a Florida retirement community. Before making a commitment, I suggest you rent until you're comfortable and confident with both your location and your finances.

People work hard their entire lives to build a nest egg. It's up to each household to decide how and where to live during their golden years. Some may want to remain in their homes; others may want to settle into a special retirement community. The more adventurous may even want to buy an RV and travel the country.

Whatever your passion may be, a large nest egg gives you the opportunity to really live and enjoy your retirement years rather than just living them out. Building an adequate nest egg offers you a wide range of options.

Being older also opens many doors to discounted prices. I was reminded of this the other day when I was offered to pay the senior rate at a nearby movie theater.

In the past, I've stated that one of my personal goals is to visit and hike as many of our national parks as possible. For people over 62, our National Parks System offers a tremendous value; a lifetime pass to all 59 U.S. National Parks for a one-time fee of just $10.

Like so many other things, however, the price is increasing to $80 at the end of August. If you're currently 62 or older, I suggest you take advantage of the current price immediately. It can be processed on the Internet for a $10 fee; still far less than the September hike to $80.

Retirement may take you down many roads, but I suggest you won't find any more beautiful or enjoyable roads than those that lead to our magnificent national parks.

Ken Morris
As seen in Oakland Press 1/21/18

Why your retirement plans may not pan out.

There are several publications that provide a list of "Top Tens" for retirees. There are the top ten places to live as a retiree; the top ten places where you can live just on your Social Security check; and, of course, the top ten vacation spots. It seems like almost everyone welcomes retirees along with their disposable income.

In reality, there are numerous retirees with a sizeable nest egg that aren't going anywhere soon, and it's not because they're hurting in the pocketbook. The reason is that they're either responsible for an aging parent or a sick spouse.

As I was reviewing the year-end reports for my clients' accounts, I discovered that many of them are shouldering the responsibility for a loved one. That doesn't just mean care and welfare; in some instances, it also means chipping in financially.

Study after study tries to determine how much money retirees will spend on health care related matters, including Medicare premiums. The consensus of these studies suggests that they will spend in excess of $250,000.

The well-respected Nationwide Retirement Institute found that Americans are "terrified" of health care costs in retirement. In fact, a recent poll of adults aged 50 and older found that 69 percent of pre-retirees listed health care costs as their number one concern in retirement.

Not that many years ago, I wrote about parents that were funding their children's education while at the same time setting dollars aside for their own retirement.

Fast forward to today. Those same parents have achieved the goal of educating their kids and are now either retired or on the cusp. They should be able to enjoy a carefree retirement. But, wait a minute. Now there's another responsibility.

Now their aging parents or a suddenly seriously ill spouse needs to be taken care of. And that can require just as much time and money as raising children. Possibly more.

What I have found so uplifting is that those clients I know who are foregoing some of the fun and sun of retirement to take care of a loved one are shouldering the responsibility without complaint.

As we begin 2018, I strongly encourage everyone who is working to continue to save for retirement. But please understand that all those retirement dollars aren't likely to be just for fun and travel.

You're likely to find that you'll need some of that money for the care of a spouse. Or maybe your own parents might turn to you for financial assistance or need you to be their primary caregiver.

Such issues can put a real damper on your plans to winter in Florida or relocate to Costa Rica. And you can forget about any river cruises down the Danube. As mentioned, I'm proud and pleased that so many of my clients are willingly foregoing the fun.

I often say that a big part of financial planning is planning for the unexpected. Perhaps major health care costs in retirement used to be unexpected. But, today it's often a reality.

Nobody can predict the future, but as people live longer and longer, it demands two things. Time and money. Retirement just might not be glamorous and it will likely take a lot more money than you initially projected. Don't be taken by surprise.

CHAPTER **6**

Losses

Ken Morris
As seen in the Oakland Press
6-19-06

Fight volatility by moving your assets.

The recent volatility in the investment world is one of the reasons I 've been such an outspoken proponent of diversification. The Nasdaq Index recently fell 8 trading days in a row, and both the DJIA and S&P 500 Index have moved like a roller coaster at Cedar Point. Looking at your investment account every day can get depressing. You begin to think the unthinkable, like selling all the securities you own and putting the money under your mattress. Everywhere you look, all you see and is doom and gloom. Even the business channels, which are notoriously pro-market, have very few words of encouragement. No wonder people are depressed.

Suddenly, it seems like the markets turn around and jump like a jackrabbit based on some inconsequential world event or an offhanded comment by a Federal Reserve official. Looking back, in other words, there was no apparent reason for the torturous downturn or the sudden spike.

The emotions of an up and down investment climate can really take a toll on one's nerves. Too many people sell every time they hear something negative, then try to buy back in on the slightest positive news. Attempting to time the market is not a good idea. It's far too risky. That's why I suggest for most investors that, rather than constantly buying and selling, they should rely on asset allocation. I am not suggesting that changes should never be made, because reviews and rebalancing are definitely important. But I am suggesting that most investors should keep their emotions out of their investment decisions, and a good way to accomplish this is simply to practice asset allocation.

Another negative side effect of all this volatility is that it tends to scare some people away, especially those who may be new to investing in the market. I would encourage everyone to keep contributing to their retirement accounts, regardless of what's happening throughout the world and during perceived periods of gloom and doom. History and past performances have shown us that, quite often, the negativity perceived by the majority can provide an good buying opportunity for those with the opposite point of view.

In summary, I would suggest that investors ignore the short-term volatility of the market and to keep a focus on their long-term goals and objectives. Yes, this often requires nerves of steel and an iron stomach, but the past few weeks has been a good example of why I strongly encourage the use of asset allocation.

Ken Morris
As seen in the Oakland Press
3-16-08

In down markets, think percentages, not dollars.

I've received numerous e-mails that essentially asked the same question: "Ken, is this the worst you have ever seen?" From an investment perspective, the answer is simply: "Not yet." So far this year, most of the major market indexes are down by double-digit percentages. In 1987, the market lost 20 percent in a single day. The memories of that particular downturn will remain with me forever. Our current plunge likely isn't over, and while most investors have been through worse, it's easy to see why this one appears to be the worst ever.

When talking about money, we tend to think in terms of hard dollar amounts. For instance, we know the price of a gallon of gasoline, the annual cost of college tuition and the amount we take home in our paycheck. But, in this day and age, with so many prices inflated, we need to factor a second part into our equation. Rather than just dollars, we need to begin thinking in terms of percentages

What's the difference? Well, I've recently spoken to several people who claim they lost the most money they've ever lost since they started investing. In dollar amounts this may be true, but not necessarily as a percentage.

For example, let's say a retired man with a nest egg of $250,000 gets $12,500 of it wiped out. Certainly he's upset that the account is down, but he's also concerned that it's even more than he lost back in 1987. That's true of the dollar amount, but in percentage terms, probably not.

Let me clarify. Suppose in 1987 that account was worth $100,000. A loss of 10 percent back then would have been $10,000, clearly less than today's $12,500. But bring history and mathematics into the equation and we have s different picture.

After the 1987 downturn, our guy enjoyed the benefits of an historic bull market. In all likelihood, he also made additional deposits into his retirement nest egg. Now for the mathematics. On a $100,000 nest egg, a 10 percent loss would be $10,000. But a 10 percent loss on his $250,000 nest egg would have been $25,000. Suddenly, the $12,500 loss, a 5 percent drop, doesn't seem so bad.

The point is we have to frame our thinking. Nobody likes to take a backward step. On the surface, a $12,500 loss seems like a lot, but when you put your mind into the proper framework, it shouldn't create a panic. Saying you lost 5 percent doesn't sound as bad as saying you're down $12,500.

In all probability, the size of the average nest egg today is larger than it was in 1987. Mentally, it's only going to become more difficult as inflation pushes up the costs of goods and we're dealing with larger and larger numbers. Our minds tend to think in terms of Washingtons, Lincolns and Franklins. But as nest eggs get larger and prices escalate, we need to add the mathematical skills of Jefferson into the equation and also think in terms of percentages.

If we don't start thinking that way, the dollar amounts will become so large it will be difficult to put everything into perspective. This could make it difficult to properly understand our losses and gains and lead to questionable financial decisions.

—⊂∞⊃—

Ken Morris
As seen in the Oakland Press
3-23-08

All your eggs in one basket?
One fall can crack them all.

The employees of Bear Stearns will always remember St. Patrick's Day 2008. Unfortunately, it won't be for the green beer and laughter, but rather for the one day that changed so many of its employees' lives. Between Friday and Monday, the value of the firm's stock fell more than 90 percent. The stock opened Monday morning at just $2 per share. There will be articles written for years on what happened and why, but the bottom line is that about one-half of the 14,000 employees are suddenly looking for work. What saddens me most, however, is that so many well-educated, financially astute individuals failed to follow one of the basic foundations of financial planning, diversification.

One interviewee said that 17 years of savings for his children's college education disappeared overnight and another expressed shock that his retirement nest egg was virtually wiped out. Anyone who thought he or she was an astute investor was lamenting buying the stock on Friday for $32 per share. Naturally, all these stories are very unfortunate, but again, this is a real life reminder to my readers why I continually preach the importance of diversification. Never, under any circumstances should you put all your eggs in one basket.

Locally, I'm sure many of you remember the K-Mart debacle. A lot of people lost a lot of money, and they were significant losses. Who could ever forget the shell games at Enron that resulted in substantial losses to both stockholders and employees? It's no secret that our own car companies are struggling for a variety of reasons. Sadly, their share prices, too, are not even close to their previous peaks. Simply stated, there are numerous reasons why a person should never put their entire financial future in the hands of just one company's stock. A Bear market brings share prices down, but bankruptcy, or in the case of Bear Stearns, a takeover to prevent a likely bankruptcy, is really bad news, especially if you happen to own that particular stock. Everyone wants to be a Microsoft millionaire or pick up some shares of the next Google before it skyrockets. But, is it worth putting the kids' entire college fund at risk? Do you want to put yourself in a situation where the only way you can possibly make it in retirement is if you win a class action lawsuit? These are definitely not financial circumstances you want to find yourself in.

Diversification may be boring. It is seldom very glamorous and it's rarely the best way to turn you into an overnight millionaire. But it will never make the headlines because it caused your retirement assets to disappear in the blink of an eye. Because, in most situations, it's a major contributing factor toward financial stability and peace of mind. I would rather have a large portion of college tuition accounted for than have nothing set aside at all. I would rather have to watch my discretionary spending during retirement than be in a situation where I could not even consider retirement. If all your eggs are in one basket, your goals and dreams can go down the drain in a heartbeat. If you diversify, the odds are very slim that you will lose everything. And the first rule of winning is not losing.

Ken Morris
As seen in the Oakland Press
6-29-08

Don't give in to capitulation.

It's difficult to believe, but here we are at the halfway point of the calendar year. From an economic standpoint, there aren't a lot of happy people these days. Four dollar per gallon gasoline has certainly had an adverse domino effect throughout the country. Manufactures have seen a dramatic increase in the cost of getting their goods to market.

Buyers feel the pinch of increased energy costs and the resultant decrease in disposable income for discretionary spending. In other words, consumers are not spending and producers are not selling at anticipated levels. And while economic conditions have been pretty poor for the first half of the year, there is little reason to be optimistic about the second half.

One word you may be seeing and hearing quite a bit in the near term is "capitulation." Capitulation is the point at which stocks are so oversold that they appear to be great bargains for purchasers. I have often mentioned how difficult it is to time the market by picking the tops and bottoms. Capitulation is the point in time when investors feel compelled to sell. They feel total despair and are willing to unload their holdings at any price they can get. Sadly, distress selling based on emotion is often a decision that many will regret in the long term.

Right now, it appears that most investors are keeping their emotions in check. Even though most market indexes are down by double digits at the mid-year point, there appears to be a minimal amount of the kind of panic selling that results in capitulation. But what happens if the markets fall another 10 or 20 percent? Will we see a wave of panic selling and capitulation?

When we reach the point of capitulation, investors will start selling like they've heard the starter's pistol at a track meet.

As I said, they may regret it later. But there is an upside to the story, Historically, capitulation is an indicator that the market is bottoming out and ready to turn around; that a new bull market may be about to begin. As I have often said, though, we can learn a lot from history, but it's no guarantee of the future.

So far, we have not seen the kind of panic selling that often leads to capitulation. I sincerely hope that we don't see panic in the market, because too many people will be hurt financially and the emotions involved in selling at a loss are not very healthy for anyone. Whether it's a stock or a home, people simply don't like seeing their assets go up in smoke.

So, are there any good investment opportunities today? Quite possibly. But it's extremely difficult to pick individual winners in an environment like this. Don't jump at a stock just because it's low by historical standards. Right now, countless stocks are way off their highs.

Years from now when we look back, some stocks that are low now low will still be low. Others may be significantly higher. The important thing is to keep your emotions at bay, whether you're a seller or a buyer. The investors that come out ahead are likely to be those that can maintain their composure while others are being driven by emotion.

Ken Morris
As seen in the Oakland Press
10-12-08

What's your plan to get through this financial storm?

As Michiganders, we're used to wild fluctuations in our weather. As the saying goes, "If you don't like the weather, just wait five minutes, because in all likelihood, it's going to change."

Unfortunately, in recent weeks the investment world has been much like the Michigan weather. It's essentially been unpredictable. Lately, though, it hasn't experienced something that the Michigan weather often gives us. It's been quite a while since we've seen one of those suddenly beautiful, sunshiny days.

Simply stated, the weather in the investment world is a torrential downpour and it seems to be getting worse. Without a doubt, the difference between the unpredictable Michigan weather and the investment climate is that the economic problems we're facing are man made.

There's plenty of blame to go around. Politicians of both parties have contributed to the problems in the form of weak policies, lack of oversight and the inability to tackle difficult issues. What's more, the private sector has its own share of issues, not the least of which is excessive executive compensation by struggling companies.

The bottom line is that the economic meltdown is being fueled by a crisis in confidence. The ramifications of the banks' reticence to lend money have a domino effect.

The banks not only lack the confidence to do business with each other, they're reluctant to do business with corporate America as well. As a result, the moms and dads of America and the young students trying to get themselves through college have nowhere to turn for financing.

Banks, which are supposed to be the economic lubricants of the economy, have simply dried up. Money is staying in the banks.

What we're left with are investments whose values have, to put it mildly, taken a pounding. After the roller coaster ride of October 6, nearly half of the stocks that make up the Standard & Poor's 500 Index were trading at their 52-week low.

This is indeed a confirmation of what we probably already knew. Almost every family in America, and especially Michigan, is facing some very major financial problems. Everyone is talking about what needs to be done in the face of this crisis. In fact, not much can be done. If you're caught in rainstorm and you're soaking wet, there's little need to open an umbrella. The reality is that everyone's anxiety is legitimate and real.

Those still in the workforce should continue to contribute to their retirement programs. Hopefully, you'll be able to look back someday and realize your contributions during this downturn were actually made at bargain prices. After all, it is better to buy low.

All households, especially those with retirees, should review your spending. Try not to touch your nest egg. Taking out dollars in a down period has the potential to do irreparable long-term harm to your balance.

One key item that every household should commit to in 2009 is to prepare a financial plan. This downturn has thrown a huge monkey wrench into just about everyone's financial planning. We need to readjust our plans to the reality of today's values. In essence, we've all been knocked down. We all need to stand up, dust ourselves off, take financial inventory and determine what long-term impact this financial storm has delivered to our financial futures.

Ken Morris
As seen in the Oakland Press
10-26-08

A bold prediction about the duration of this downtown.

It doesn't matter whether I'm talking to existing clients or checking e-mails from readers, the same two questions keep popping up. "Have you ever seen anything like this before?" And "How long do you think this will last before things turn around?

All one has to do is turn on the television to see a wide range of experts discussing our nation's financial woes. As I have previously written, many fingers have been pointing to the cause, but it is for certain that our economy today is quite ill. The government has put forth numerous remedies, but as I write this column, the medicine has barely begun to enter into the nation's bloodstream.

As a seasoned advisor, I've been through many downturns. I clearly recall the one-day 20 percent drop in 1987. In 1990, we had the downturn fueled by the Savings and Loan fiasco. And more recently, the tech wreck decimated many portfolios. To be honest, I've experienced several downturns, but I have never experienced anything as severe as what we are in now.

One big difference with this downturn is the amount of public anger the crisis has generated. The anger appears to be directed toward two separate entities. One recipient is Wall Street with all its greed, exorbitant bonuses and golden parachutes. The other target of the anger is our elected officials and their perceived incompetence and continual bickering.

Obviously, this is not a scientific poll, but rather, my conclusion based on talking to hundreds of experienced investors. One could argue the validity of my conclusion, but I listen to tirades from the moms and dads of America virtually every day.

As with many previous downturns, there is also fear in the air, but the anger in this crisis is something new. I believe falling housing prices have also contributed heavily to the anger. In previous downturns, I often heard people say "I should have sold my tech stock when they were up and bought real estate, because real estate never goes down."

Real estate seemed to be the one asset class Americans could count on to appreciate. Financial advisors everywhere tried to point out that it could go down, but housing had such an incredible long-term run-up that many people were convinced that it would never stop rising. Sadly, this current downturn has bluntly pointed out that stocks aren't the only assets that can go down.

Downturns have a way of changing dreams and altering goals. I believe that everyone needs to reevaluate their circumstances and make adjustments accordingly. Save whenever possible and be watchful of your spending.

So yes, I have experienced downturns, but this one is certainly different and much more severe. Unfortunately, it appears to be a self-inflicted wound. Still, I firmly believe we'll get the economy turned around. We will likely see some corporate executives punished and confirm that some elected officials were asleep.

But the economy is resilient and I expect some signs of life before the end of the year. Next year will be pivotal, but I believe we will get the economy pointed in the right direction. While I seldom make predictions, I'm confident the economy and the investment world will bounce back long before the Lions win a playoff game.

Ken Morris
As seen in Oakland Press 10/29/17

What worries Ken more than a market downturn?

I was recently asked what keeps me awake at night. Believe me, there is always enough going on this world that, if you stopped and really thought about it, should give you plenty of cause to worry.

There are hot spots all over the world that could ignite at any time. Of course I'm concerned about them, but many people believe that my biggest fear would be a sudden downturn in the stock market. After all,

I'm in the financial services industry.

But no, that isn't it at all.

Early in my career I survived a one-day, twenty percent stock market meltdown. Not only did I prevail, I successfully guided my clients through the aftermath as well. In fact, those that followed my advice didn't just survive; they thrived.

The key lesson from that October 1987 debacle is to keep your emotions at bay. You should not let them take control of your financial decisions. Because of that lesson and my experience with the 1987 downturn, I no longer fear a sharp market decline.

In fact, to a certain degree market downturns can be a positive event as they can open the door to some excellent investment opportunities. So, no, I don't lose sleep over a bad day on Wall Street.

What does concern me the most is debt. When I prepare a financial plan for a household, I always cringe when I see credit card debt. For too many, running up credit card debt is a way of life. It's buy now and figure out how to pay for it later.

In my mind, Uncle Sam is setting a poor example. The national debt is now in excess of $20 trillion and estimated to be in excess of $24 trillion by the end of 2018. Those numbers are so large; it's difficult to comprehend.

To put them into context, let's look at them as time. If I were to ask how long ago was 1,000 seconds, the answer would be 17 minutes. A million seconds ago would be 11 days, and 1 billion seconds ago takes us all the way back to 1985.

But a trillion seconds ago is like Star Trek time travel because that would take us back to 30,000 BC, which I believe is pre-dinosaur. Imagine, if you can, where 20 trillion seconds would put us. And we're more than of $20 trillion in debt.

Debt is not exclusive to our Uncle Sam. The recent hurricane in Puerto Rico brought their financial issues to the forefront. Several states across the country are on the brink of financial collapse. Similarly, numerous pension plans, both public and private, are significantly underfunded.

So it isn't just personal debt that concerns me; it's debt at all levels. All levels of government, federal, state and local, are spending well beyond their means. Pension programs, though well intentioned, have made promises they will difficulty keeping.

As a financial advisor, I know the math has to work. A politician cannot make two plus two equal five. A pension has to be financially sound to prevent a broken promise.

Environmentalists always say think green for the sake of our kids and grandkids. As a financial advisor, I also believe we should think green. By staying out of the red.

CHAPTER 7

Reasons to be optimistic. "B-positive."

Ken Morris
As seen in the Oakland Press
1-4-05

Nobody can predict the market, but anybody can diversify.

On television, in the print media or just about anywhere you look, there are headlines regarding someone's predictions for 2005. People in the financial field, like me, are constantly asked some variation of the question, "Where do you think the stock market will go this year"? Often, I find that the response is based on certain current events. A good example is what we saw last year with the elections. Remember those articles that named the stocks that would take off if Kerry won, or the stocks you should sell if Bush lost. Predictions just seem to be a part of our national fabric.

As 2005 begins, I think you should all ask yourselves whether your investment portfolio is based on predictions or on sound principles. If it is based on predictions, your buying and selling might very well be controlled by speculation, fear and greed. In the not too distant past, there was a lot of speculation on Internet stocks. Locally, there was a great deal of speculation on K-Mart, and even though it survived, most stockholders were left with very little or nothing at all. I firmly believe that, if your investment strategy is based on predictions, it's time to change your ways. Beyond a doubt, I believe a principled approach is the direction that most people should take when investing.

One principled method of investing is simply to own a well-diversified portfolio of investments. One that doesn't chase investment returns, but rather maintains a disciplined approach to long term investing. Since no one can predict with any certainty which segment of the market will perform the best, it's just common sense that diversification puts you in the best position to ultimately be successful. Obviously it enables you to avoid precipitous drops in any given sector ride. In other words, it minimizes extreme risks and enables you to ride smoothly over any potholes, basically because it assures that none of the potholes are too large All in all, a diversified portfolio has a far better chance of surviving turbulent times or miscalculated projections.

My suggestion is to start out 2005 with discipline. Avoid paying too much attention to current events and predictions. Structure your portfolio so that your investments are spread among various asset classes. If you need assistance, seek a professional advisor. I think the price of not diversifying and trying to pick the right investment at the right time is impossible for most. Don't chase returns based on predictions. In short, diversify.

Ken Morris
As seen in the Oakland Press
7-6—08

Americans will make it through tough times.

As a nation, we just celebrated the anniversary of our Independence. Unfortunately, many people tend to take our freedom for granted. and do not comprehend the price many have paid so that we can today live in a free society. There is no question that, from an economic perspective, many feel added financial stress in this day and age of $4 per gallon gasoline, job loss and simply a general feeling of financial insecurity. One only has to look at our nation's history to see that we have as a nation have a way of overcoming adversity and I am confident that once again good ol' American ingenuity will prevail and get us back on solid financial footing.

There is no question that inflation is once again in the headlines. As consumers, we are constantly seeing the costs of goods and services increasing virtually every day. This not only impacts our day- to-day lifestyles, but it also impacts our long term retirement planning. A recent study by Barclays in San Francisco concluded that about half of the middle class is underestimating their retirement needs. I would not be surprised if this estimate is actually too low. I say this because many who viewed their primary residence as a piggy bank will find that at the time of retirement when they intend to downsize that they probably will not get as much out of their home as they initially projected. Add to this the problems with Medicare insolvency and the anticipated under funding of Social Security and inflation there will be a lot of Americans that could be in for a real shock when they reach retirement age. Add a shrinking investment portfolio into the equation and you have a lot of nervous people. In other words, with all that is occurring throughout the country it is going to take a lot more money to maintain a comfortable retirement lifestyle than one would have imagined just a few short years ago.

My message today is that I realize many today are living paycheck to paycheck. Unfortunately, because of inflation that paycheck does not go as far as it did just a few short months ago. The struggles are real. The good news is that in spite of our current financial problems and the projected financial issues that still have to be resolved, that we are still the greatest country in the world. In our history at times of crisis there have been men and women who have stood up to the challenges. I am confident that within ten years there will be a new household name that today is just starting today in someones garage. The next Microsoft or Google will be a company that helps solve some of our current energy issues or perhaps even some of our environmental concerns. Whatever it is I am confident because of our personal freedoms and economic system that fosters growth that American ingenuity will once again prevail . and that the gloom and doom will fade and American optimism will return and we will once again be able to focus on achieving the retirement dream.

Ken Morris
As seen in the Oakland Press
2-2-09

Don't let the mud turn into quicksand

As I sat down to relax on a recent cold day, I turned on the television and started flipping through the news channels. All I could find were stories about the troubled economy. It eerily reminded me of the movie Groundhog Day as the same negative stories kept repeating over and over.

I was in no frame of mind to listen to all the negative reports, so I switched to one of my favorites, The History Channel. Wouldn't you know, the show was about the Great Depression and the many similarities it had to our current economic condition. At that point I felt compelled to stick with the History Channel.

Unquestionably, there are similarities, but there are also some significant differences. By way of illustration, imagine that people during the Great Depression were stuck in mud up to their shoulders,

I see the current situation as everyone stuck in the mud up to their knees.

The question is will we continue to sink or be pulled safely out. While nobody knows for sure, I believe Mark Twain said it best:

"History does not repeat itself, but it rhymes."

The pain we've seen firsthand in Michigan for many years has spread not only throughout the nation, but throughout the world. The stock market, which is a good future indicator, has had an extremely rough start this year. According to the Stock Trader's Almanac, January is often a good indicator of the general direction of the stock market. Based on history, a poor January is not a real good sign of things to come.

It's hard not to be a pessimist these days. With jobs being lost, homes be foreclosed and the constant bombardment of negative economic news it's quite easy. The negativity feeds on itself and before you realize it, doom and gloom has spread everywhere. As a financial advisor, I'm looking at 2009 as a year of financial survival. That means helping people get the most out of every dollar and every opportunity. In a downturn, financial survival means staying current with your cash flow. Don't run up credit card debt and stay current with your bills, especially the mortgage payment. If you find yourself borrowing to make ends meet, seek help immediately, not six months from now when you're drowning in debt. Financial fear is in the air, and in many ways, the general media are flaming the fire of panic.

I wish I could say that if the groundhog sees its shadow, the worst is over, but I can't. There is no on foolproof indicator of the future. But staying positive is a good idea. Don't worry about what you can't control.

I believe many people are up to the challenge. For example, more than 50 laid off autoworkers are now enrolled in Oakland University's nursing program. When faced with the unthinkable, you can drown in self-pity or step up and face a new challenge. Many of us have ancestors who fled their native land for economic reasons and made lives for themselves in the USA.

Many will need to reinvent themselves and perhaps relocate. But trying something is better than just watching all the negative news and waiting for something to happen. We may just be in a severe recession or the Great Depression II. But whatever it's ultimately called, I'm confident we will realize that this is still the greatest nation in the world.

Ken Morris
As seen in The Oakland Press 2/10/13

Stick with retirement savings, in good and bad times

There are a few exceptions, including Apple, but for the most part, equities are starting out the year quite well. Not surprisingly, seeing positive results on investment statements tends to put investors in a more positive mood.

I've often said that investors need an iron stomach to get through difficult bumps along the financial road. I guess you could say that investors are now seeing the benefits of sticking with their financial game plans.

If investments are beginning to turn positive with the economy moving at a relatively mild pace, imagine how they could explode if the economy were to begin humming at a pace we haven't seen in many years.

Even though smiles are beginning to return to investors' faces,

I actually feel badly for a significant number of them. That's because it's estimated that nearly one quarter of the monies in retirement accounts was taken out in 2012.

Many IRA holders were compelled to withdraw cash to meet their financial obligations. Maybe it was an emergency, a loss of job, or just catching up on day-to-day bills. For the same reasons, many 401(k) owners took loans against their retirement accounts.

These are not moves that I would ordinarily recommend. Unfortunately, when the bill collector calls, sometimes you have to do what you have to do.

The sad part of the story is that dollars destined for retirement purposes changed course and were used to pay current expenses.

As I indicated, this is an unfortunate situation.

Without going too heavily into the tax code, dollars that are pulled out of an IRA account early are not only subject to taxation as ordinary income, but also could be subject to tax penalties for early withdrawal.

If you were to take a loan from your 401(k), you would likely be paying a fairly high interest rate. Then when you repaid the loan, it would be with after-tax dollars. But the real misfortune of this scenario is simply that the monies are no longer there, invested for your retirement.

Obviously, any money that's not sitting comfortably in a retirement account has missed this recent growth spurt. The end result is double whammy. An opportunity lost.

It's quite apparent that pension plans are becoming a thing of the past. At the same time, the future of Social Security as we know it is, well, not secure. That's why it's imperative that everyone should save for retirement beyond the traditional retirement programs.

And when I say save, I not only mean setting the money aside, but also to keeping it set aside.

To emphasize my point, a recent study by the Employee Benefit Research Institute found that Social Security was the primary source of retirement income for 69 percent of retired Americans. The original intent of Social Security was to be a supplement, not the primary source of retirement income.

So please, stick with your retirement savings in both good and turbulent times. Retirement funds are not meant for emergencies or rainy days. They're intended for the long haul, so that Social Security won't be your primary source of retirement revenue.

Somehow, someway, those dollars dedicated to retirement need to remain in retirement accounts until you're out of the work force. Set them aside and keep them there.

Ken Morris
As seen in The Oakland Press 4/14/13

Reinstating the Civilian Conservation Corps (CCC)

Regular readers of this column know of my fondness for history, especially that of our own nation. I believe we can learn much about where we're headed by remembering what we've experienced in the past.

Buried in various news publications, you can often find "what happened this day in history." At the end of March, our nation celebrated an important milestone that impacted the finances and worth ethic of countless families throughout America. When I became aware of this, I felt I should bring it to the attention of my readers.

You see, eighty years ago, shortly after he was first elected to office, President Franklin D. Roosevelt established the Civilian Conservation Corps (CCC). I was shocked that I saw absolutely no mention of this in any publication. It made me wonder how many people out there don't even know about the CCC.

In the early 1930s, unemployment was incredibly high and the outlook for jobs growth was bleak. The CCC was initially intended for young men between the ages of 18 to 25. It wasn't military, but the men lived in barracks and there was a sort of regimentation. Those who were in charge were referred to as "Sir."

The men signed up for a six-month term and the program limited them to a maximum of four terms. The essential requirement of the men was simply to work hard. In exchange, they received $30 per month.

Of this $30, the government mandated that they send $22 to $25 home to their families every month. Based on the Consumer Price Index, published by the U.S. Bureau of Labor Statistics, that $30 per month is equivalent to $530 in today's dollars. Although desertion was a persistent problem, three million young men went through the program.

So, what did the CCC do? They built 125,000 miles of roads, constructed nearly 47,000 bridges, built 3,000 lookout fire towers, strung nearly 89,000 miles of telephone wire and planted 3 billion trees.

In addition, they fought fires, built hiking trails and excavated canals. The CCC program was a real part of our American history. It provided many young men an income and an opportunity to feel good about themselves.

Not to get into politics, but when the original stimulus program was presented to us, I envisioned a modern day CCC. Evidently, I was wrong.

Could a structured program that requires hard work and mandates money be sent home exist in our nation today?

I seriously doubt it. I'm guessing we'd take this simple one-size-fits-all program and turn it into something extremely complex. For example, we'd probably have exceptions to the regimented lifestyle. And I suspect that the workforce would have to wait for permits and environmental studies before undertaking many of the projects.

Our nation's history is filled with issues that were pocketbook related. Unfortunately, many of them are overlooked in our history books. The CCC was a simple concept that benefited many young men and their families during the Depression.

The CCC should not be buried in our history books. Many young men were taught the work ethic, the value of a hard day's work and the importance of helping out family. There are financial lessons in the CCC, not only for families, but also for politicians. Especially for politicians.

Ken Morris
As seen in Oakland Press 10/16/16

Are you missing out on the best value in America?

There was a lot of hype prior to the first presidential debate. Now all the political experts and pollsters are rehashing it and telling us who won. If I had been home, I definitely would have watched it. But since I was on vacation I missed it.

I didn't visit a luxurious European capital or cruise to an exotic Caribbean Island. But by no means would you categorize my vacation as ordinary. Because I visited and hiked our five majestic National Parks in Utah.

I think former president Theodore Roosevelt deserves far more recognition than he has already received. He launched our nation's National Parks Program. There's a lot of spectacular landscape throughout our country and it's nice to know it will remain that way.

In recognition of our National Park program's 100th anniversary, commemorative stamps and coins are now available through the U.S. Post Office and Mint. I find it remarkable that anyone over 62 can get a lifetime pass good at all the National Parks for just $10.

If an amusement park offered such a bargain, people would line up for hours. I almost feel guilty going into a park and keeping money in my pocket. It just may be the best value in America. And even though attendance is up, I don't believe enough people take advantage of this incredible benefit.

Why mention national parks in a financial column? Because they're an outstanding value and because our society puts such an emphasis on health. I can't think of a more pleasant way to stay healthy than by visiting and hiking within a park and enjoying the great outdoors.

There's a saying that you need good health to enjoy your wealth. There are a lot of people, myself included, that believe monthly gym dues are money well spent. I also think it's great that we have outstanding biking and walking trails, funded by many of our local municipalities.

But there's nothing quite like the beauty of our National Parks.

According to the most recent U.S. Government data, the national parks had 292 million visitors in 2014, many of which were foreign tourists. These visitors generate over 275, 000 private sector jobs in surrounding communities and it's estimated that the parks generate $30 billion in economic activity.

In other words, surrounding hotels, restaurants and other businesses look forward to park visitors each and every year. The federal government estimates that every dollar invested in The National Park Service generates $10 in economic activity.

The government spends a lot of money on programs that I personally disagree with and do not support. I think most tax dollars that go to Washington are inefficiently spent.

I was alarmed to learn that, of all the tax dollars we send to Uncle Sam, only one fifteenth of one percent is earmarked for funding our National Parks program. I think it's sad that only a tiny sliver goes into operating and maintaining one of our nation's greatest treasures.

During the next presidential debate, I wish the moderator would ask the candidates when was the last time they visited a National Park and what improvements they would like to see.

I have a feeling that if this question were ever asked, the candidates would respond with nothing but dead silence.

Ken Morris
As seen in Oakland Press 11/6/16

It doesn't matter who wins.

The political finish line is within sight, and in the opinion of many of my readers, it can't get here soon enough. I heartily agree. What's more, I can't help feeling that when I wake up Wednesday morning I'll be disappointed no matter who wins.

I'm fairly certain that, regardless of the winner, our nation's capital will continue its dysfunctional and fiscally irresponsible ways. For me, however, it's time to set aside my frustrations with our political system.

Regular readers know I like to say that, when it comes to investing, it's important to keep your emotions in check. I believe this attitude should also carry over to one's feelings about political elections.

This is an opportune time to be appreciative of the fact that, in spite of all of our flaws, this is still the greatest country on the planet. I submit that there are plenty of reasons for financial optimism.

The peaceful change of leadership is the American way and that's one of the reasons I feel my initial disappointment will soon turn into optimism. Regardless of who's sitting in the Oval Office, I'm pretty sure I'll still be able to pull into a service station, fill my tank and get a coffee for a dollar.

The malls will be open to shop and banks will be open for business. I could go on with examples, but I'm sure you get the idea. Life will go on as normal for most of us, and our future will remain bright. True, there will likely be higher taxes, more business red tape, and higher overall costs. But at the end of the day, thanks to technological advances, I'm very optimistic.

It seems like I have a client sit in my office almost every day and describe a recent medical procedure that's beyond belief. A friend whose legs were paralyzed fourteen years ago in an accident is now walking with braces controlled by a high tech belt. He's traveling the world, demonstrating the technology and seeking investors for the manufacturer.

I recently read about software firms that are committed to battling cancer. During the summer I attended an outdoor wedding and the photographer used a drone to capture the ceremony.

My grandchildren will never know there used to be a telephone where you couldn't see the person on the other end. And, of course, there are automobiles capable of going down the road without a driver.

Do you know what all these examples have in common? They all offer some kind of investment opportunity. Without question, investing has an element of risk, but there's also tremendous potential to solve problems, improve lives and make money.

Innovation is one of the reasons I'm turning from political frustration to economic optimism. Hopefully, Washington will not choke innovation because I believe we're on the cusp of some incredible discoveries. And the companies behind them offer investment potential that could enrich your portfolio.

Politicians promise to solve all our problems, but once elected they often have different agendas. Most people realize it's on their own shoulders, not Uncle Sam's to achieve their financial objectives. I've personally decided to live by my blood type, which is B positive. Regardless of your blood type, there's good reason for you to be positive too.

CHAPTER 8

Financial Stuff.

Ken Morris
As seen in the Oakland Press
6-22-08

Investing: read the small print.

Developed in the 1940's at the University of Michigan, the Index of Consumer Sentiment gives a fairly reliable indication of the future actions of stocks, bonds, and the dollar.

In June of 1980, under the Carter administration, that consumer sentiment hit a low of 58.7. Twenty eight years later, the index has hit another low. After averaging 85.6 throughout 2007, the index dropped to 59.8 in May, and then to 56.7 this month. At two full points lower than the previous low, that's not an optimistic sign.

Interestingly, the negative sentiment in both instances was "fueled" by oil. Every time you pull out your wallet these days, it seems like you're paying more than you were just a few months ago. Once again, the primary reason is the increasing cost of energy that's being passed on to the consumer.

As a nation, we consume nearly 21 million barrels of oil per day. To put it into perspective, that translates into 26 percent of the daily *worldwide* consumption. In a nutshell, the problem is simple: We're consuming more and producing less and less of our own oil. So the price increase is mainly the result of the imbalance between supply and demand. It's also the primary reason behind the plummeting consumer sentiment.

The increasing cost of energy is why alternatives to oil, commonly referred to as alternative energy, have been at the forefront of the news.

Nuclear energy is a viable and misunderstood energy resource. Nationally, we have the largest capacity of any nation at just over 100,000 megawatts. France follows at just over 63,000 megawatts. There's no question that, as the price of oil increases, nuclear power will become more and more attractive. Unfortunately, a permit to build a nuclear plant is a three-year process. Consequently, nuclear energy will have minimal impact in the immediate future.

Another alternative is wind energy. The famous billionaire who made his fortune in oil and natural gas recently projected that oil would be at $150 per barrel by this October. He is in the process of building one of the largest wind farms in the nation in Texas. Clearly, it appears that alternative energy is something that will remain a popular topic for some time to come.

As consumers today, we have a serious problem. We were first made aware of it in the 1970s, during the oil embargo. Unfortunately, it was a problem our elected officials ignored and never properly addressed.

As investors, we have numerous opportunities. Our own auto companies are diving headfirst into developing practical, affordable vehicles powered by alternative energy. While many hybrids are already on the road, much more work remains to make fuel cells feasible for mass production.

That's not to say investing in fuel cells is not a good idea. Opportunities also exist in nuclear power generation, uranium producers, and wind and solar energy providers. Some companies are even attempting to harness the power of ocean waves to produce electricity.

Keep in mind that investment opportunities also mean investment risk. Many people, who jumped into ethanol with emotion, but without proper research, learned the hard way that good ideas don't always produce investment gains. The big picture may look appealing, but understand that success or failure often lies within the small print.

Ken Morris
As seen in the Oakland Press
6/28/09

Unusual invest theories, correlations and myths.

In anticipation of the Red Wings winning the Stanley Cup, I began doing some financial digging to see if I could find any correlation between the investment world and the Wings winning the Cup. Unfortunately, the Wings were stunned by a flock of Penguins. Still, I thought it might be fun to look at some of the more unusual investment correlations.

After the recent misfortunes of our Wings and Lions, I felt it was time for a lighthearted message. So let's take an out-of-the-box look at some of the financial world's more wacky indicators. Under no circumstances should they be used to make actual investment decisions.

One of the better-known correlations comes from the National Football League. It states that if an original AFL team wins the Super Bowl, the stock market will be down. Using the Standard & Poor's Index as a measuring stick, in the 14 AFC wins, the market has been down on average almost 4 percent. With the 22 NFL wins, the market has been up on average over 12 percent.

This year's winner was Pittsburgh, an original NFL team. This remarkable correlation shows that after each of Pittsburgh's previous

Super Bowl wins, the stock market has performed well by most measuring sticks.

Another fun stock market indicator is the aspirin indicator. Simply stated, if aspirin sales increase, stock prices decline. Probably because, in tough difficult times like today, people feel more stress and buy more aspirin. Last year was a terrible year in the global stock markets. Not surprisingly, the sale of Advil was up 2 percent with a fourth quarter sales surge.

Still another frequently mentioned indicator is the Sports Illustrated swim suit issue. The theory goes that if the model is American, the stock market will have a positive year. If she's foreign, it will have a difficult financial year. One only has to look at 1995 to see that this myth has some serious flaws. While 1995 was a great year for most investors, the SI cover model was foreign born.

Then there's the cardboard box indicator. This one makes sense. If goods and services are being shipped, boxes should be in demand. In our current economy, most cardboard box producers posted poor performance for 2008.

Some people suggest there's a correlation between the length of skirts and investment performance. Others look for indicators in music and lipstick sales. But my favorite is the MacDonald's indicator, commonly called the Big Mac Index.

This index doesn't forecast market performance; it measures the strength of the dollar against foreign currencies. If you're planning a vacation overseas, this indicator allegedly helps you determine if your dollar is fairly priced against the foreign currency. In other words, is it over or undervalued?

I was hoping this week to applaud our repeat Stanley Cup Champion Detroit Red Wings. But in sports, just as with investments, anything can happen. What looks good on paper is not necessarily going to happen.

When it comes to investment and finances, the world is full of unusual theories, correlations and myths. None of them should ever be used to make serious financial decisions. There is no substitute for research. And even when research is thoroughly done, the actual game still has to be played.

Ken Morris
As seen in The Oakland Press 5/22/10

Putting money where you think it's safe isn't always the case.

A number of readers have contacted me wondering if there's anywhere they can put their savings that would pay higher interest than their bank account. It's a good question. Losing money on your investments is one thing, but feeling like you're losing money on what you considered to be your "safe" money is extremely unpleasant.

You may not actually be losing money, but considering taxes, the low interest rate on your savings and inflation, you may well be losing purchasing power.

So why do so many people put their safe money in the bank? The obvious answers are safety and accessibility. Your bank deposits are guaranteed; insured by the FDIC up to statutory limits. And you have almost immediate access to your money when you need it. But even though the face value of your money will never decrease, your purchasing power might. So, doesn't it make sense to look for something that can offer you better returns?

My concern is that, as people seek alternatives, some may put their money into vehicles they think are safe, but don't fully understand. I've encountered many savers who are oblivious to the fact that seeking greater returns often means greater risk. Even with such traditional investments as bonds, there's the possibility of losing principal. Fixed-income investments fluctuate in value as interest rates move up or down.

So what can you do with your money that would generally be safe and keep you ahead of where you are now?

Well, consider where a significant percentage of your money is going. Like credit card interest, often in the 20 percent range, and your car loan at about 10 percent. If you're paying high interest on money you owe, you might want to pay off that debt and stop giving someone else interest on your money.

How about paying down your mortgage? Would that make sense for you? A little math can help decide. Before you file away those federal and state income tax returns, determine your effective income tax rate by adding the percentage of tax from your both returns.

A typical effective rate is in the neighborhood of 30 percent and the interest rate on most home mortgages these days is between 5 and 6 percent. So let's suppose you have a 6 percent rate along with a 30 percent effective income tax rate.

The deductibility of mortgage interest could effectively reduce the amount of tax you have to pay on your gross income. In this case, the after tax cost of the mortgage is 4.2 percent. (30 percent of 6 percent is 1.8 percent, and 6 - 1.8 = 4.2.)

As an investor, that means you'd have to find a vehicle that delivered an after tax return better than 4.2 percent to be ahead. Yes, it is possible to find such investments.

But if you have cash sitting somewhere in an account that doesn't yield more than your after tax mortgage rate (4.2 percent in our example), I suggest you do the math. In the current low interest rate environment, this is a relatively simple idea that shouldn't be overlooked.

If the circumstances are right, prepaying your mortgage can be better than just leaving your dollars in the bank. If you're uncertain whether this strategy works for you, be sure consult your tax or financial advisor.

That's why I would like to suggest to you to look into your pockets and think about what's keeping the cash out. Where's your money going to? Are those monthly payments to your credit cards at about 20% interest keeping money out of your pocket?

Ken Morris
As seen in The Oakland Press 8/1/10

Investors beware.

Most of us are familiar with the phrase "Robbing Peter to pay Paul." Generally speaking, when we hear this, we get an image of someone struggling to decide which bills to pay and which to let slide. But way back in 1899, a con man named William Miller offered his investors an opportunity to earn a return of 10 percent per week. Not surprisingly, the scheme turned out to be fraudulent, and the phrase, "robbing Peter to pay Paul" was attached to the scam.

In 1919, Charles Ponzi began as a legitimate firm, selling postage coupons internationally to take advantage of various nations' currency values. When all was said and done, thousands of people lost their homes and life savings. Today, the scam of paying long-time investors with the money from new investors is simply known as a Ponzi scheme.

In December 2008, an international Ponzi scheme crumbled when Bernie Madoff could not find new investors to kick in the cash to pay off his large contingent of established investors. It's estimated that Madoff's "investors" lost in the neighborhood $50 billion. In all likelihood, we will never have a true and accurate number.

We do know, however, that retirement net eggs were decimated, charitable programs collapsed, and even suicides ensued. It was incredibly tragic. A con man lived a lavish lifestyle while government auditors failed to do their job.

In reality, although some will not now admit it, many investors were motivated by greed. At a time when everyday investors saw the value of their nest eggs bouncing up and down, Mr. Madoff's clients were experiencing steady returns. Returns that were simply too good to be true.

To be perfectly candid, not every investor was naïve; many were just plain greedy. And it was their greed that did them in. They can blame regulators for not uncovering Madoff's scheme, but when all is said and done, it was their greed that caused them to lose their nest egg. William Miller, Charles Ponzi and Bernard Madoff all took advantage of people who thought they could get better investment returns than anyone else.

Closer to home, it appears that many Michiganders recently fell victim to an alleged Ponzi scheme. Some 440 investors, most of them from Michigan, are out an estimated $55 million. According to a court-appointed receiver, there is little chance they will get much of it back. I just do not understand how anyone can invest sums as large as $300,000 or $500,000 without knowing substantially more about where their money is going.

I am certain that in the days to come we will hear tragic tale after tragic tale. I feel just awful for these victims, but what motivated them to turn over their life savings to a firm that was established only a few years ago? The only conclusion I can come to is investors' greed. It's a sad story that has repeated itself countless times throughout history.

It may sound simple, but investors need to be cautious and realistic. Most investment advisors are true professionals. But, as with any other profession, there are a few bad apples. Unfortunately, these criminals are not thugs, but charming, smooth-talking con men. So please, don't be greedy. Keep a level head and remain cautious and realistic.

Ken Morris
As seen in The Oakland Press 9/19/10

Investors continue to succumb to fraudulent snake oil salesmen

Most readers have probably heard of Bernie Madoff, who is currently a prison term of 125 years for running the largest Ponzi scheme in our nation's history. CNBC recently aired a program that talked about his life in prison and featured interviews with some of victims whose financial lives have been ruined forever.

Not one of the victims ever dreamed something like this could ever happen to them. But, whether it's a case of succumbing to irresistible charm, or just a typical case of financial greed, investors continue to succumb to fraudulent snake oil salesmen.

On September 2, Joseph Blimline of Dallas pleaded guilty in federal court for mail fraud. In 2004, he was just outside our state capital, making a presentation in Okemos to potential investors for his oil and gas exploration program.

This particular program, he promised eager listeners, would hand then a return of 6 percent per month. At this point, I believe a level-headed person should have noted not just one, but two red flags.

First, of course, is the astronomical 6 percent per month return. At that rate, investors would more than double their money in just 12 months. Never in my career, have I seen a legitimate investment that could come close to this kind of return.

The second red flag, probably not as obvious to the untrained ear, is the word "promise." To my way of thinking, that word, along with the word "guarantee" should always be on a potential investor's radar screen.

Just down the street from Okemos, a Mason, Michigan man by the name of Ty Klotz was sentenced to 6 ½ years in prison for money laundering. He ran a Ponzi scheme that lured investors into a "private hedge fund" that was going to net them a handsome 20 percent per month return.

Clearly, this is an outrageous claim. Such returns are literally unachievable. And yet, 352 "investors" blithely ponied up some $2.2 million. Investors? No, that's too kind. They were foolish victims who got carried away by greed. Then again, maybe they were just sadly lacking in math skills.

In this economic environment, with so many people needing to squeeze every penny, it's more important than ever for investors to be wary of scammers like Blimline and Klotz and the tentacles of greed. Regulators require that legitimate financial advisors pass exams to obtain security licenses. Regulators mandate continuing education standards and have strict rules regarding advertising and disclosures to potential investors.

In fact, it is more difficult than ever these days for a legitimate financial advisor to be in compliance with the pages and pages of rules and regulations that he or she must follow. Keep in mind that most con men are not even licensed. They totally disregard the rules and laws that legitimate advisors are required to follow.

Still, it happens time and time again. The public keeps falling victim to these unscrupulous con men. I firmly believe that a majority of these victims should know better.

But for whatever reason, greed overcomes common sense and they invest in the hope of hitting it big. Unfortunately, they will more than likely end up with nothing but shattered promises, and little or no money to show for their grief.

On March 7, 2006, the CFTC charged Ty and Monette Klotz and their two companies, Aurifex Commodities Research Company and Aurifex Research L.L.C., with fraud in operating a Ponzi-like scheme while operating and soliciting participants for what they called a "private hedge fund." On February 1, 2008, Judge Bell ordered Ty and Monette Klotz to pay more than $3.1 million in sanctions for their fraudulent conduct, which injured approximately 352 individuals who invested at least $2.2 million (see CFTC News Release 5451-08, February 8, 2008).

Ken Morris
As seen in The Oakland Press 6/12/11

Investors and technology

It's not unusual in the financial services industry to come across traveling analogies that are used to illustrate the importance of planning and investing. For example, many of us have heard such phrases as the retirement roadmap, the road to retirement, the retirement journey, and investing for the long haul.

All these expressions emphasize the importance of having a financial plan for the journey that we call life.

Over the Memorial Day holiday, my wife and I attended a wedding in upstate New York. I would like to point out that neither of us had ever been to that part of New York before.

Still, making the decision to drive all that way was not a big deal. After all, we had no reason for concern. Our good friend modern technology would certainly get us to our destination without a hitch.

With technology on our side, we didn't even bother to take one of those old-fashioned paper things called a roadmap. We simply entered our destination into our home computer and within minutes we received a detailed printout of the best route to follow. It even told us precisely how long the trip was going to take. Amazing.

In the car, we also had a GPS, where, just as with the computer, we plugged in the ultimate destination. Confidently we began our road trip, but the confidence waned a bit as we soon encountered our first problem. The printed directions from our computer and the GPS were not the same. They provided conflicting routes.

Fortunately, we had yet another piece of technology at our

disposal that would surely resolve the conflict. Our relatively new, and practically state-of-the-art cell phones had GPS capabilities.

Quickly, the route was set by our cell phone. The only problem was that rather than confirming one of our other two routes, it provided a third alternative.

Well, we ultimately arrived at our destination and enjoyed the wedding. But there are lessons to take away from our high-tech travel adventures.

In years past, it was often quite difficult to find information. In today's high-tech world, I think it's almost impossible to avoid being inundated with information. There's even a term for it: Information overload.

It can be a real challenge to sort through all the information that's so readily available in today's world. The financial services industry is no exception. There are so many sources and such volumes of financial information out there; it's essential to confirm the accuracy before acting on it.

The other financial lesson is that there are many ways to get from point A to point B. Using our journey analogy, someone might just be comfortable driving the freeways, while someone else may be more at ease using the old two-lane highways.

The same is true of investing. Once you establish your financial destination, in most instances there are several routes you can choose that allow you to comfortably get there.

In other words, in spite of what some experts say, there is more than one financial route to financial freedom. As investors, your challenge is to find the one that makes you feel most comfortable.

Technology may be helpful and it may guide you well, but it still takes human intelligence to select the best route for your own set of circumstances.

Ken Morris
As seen in The Oakland Press 9/16/12

Debt reaching $16 trillion reminds us of need to get spending under control

Labor Day weekend is the unofficial end of summer in Michigan. While many walked the Mackinac Bridge, others enjoyed various festivals throughout the state and some simply chilled and grilled.

As people traveled throughout Michigan and the rest of the country, they saw staggering gasoline prices when they pulled up to the pump. In fact, the national average for gasoline prices set an all time high for a Labor Day weekend.

Then, on the day after the Labor Day holiday, a Tuesday that felt like a Monday, our nation reached another milestone just after 4PM. The United States national debt exploded past the $16 trillion mark

That number isn't just staggering, it's almost beyond comprehension. If the debt were divided among all the households in the country, each one would owe more than $125,000. And there's absolutely no reason to believe that the trend line is going anywhere but up.

How did we get ourselves into such a hole? The answer is not overly complicated. The sad reality is we spend more than we take in as revenue. In fact, as a nation we borrow about 40 cents of every dollar we spend.

Fiscally it is frightening because it has the potential to bring our slow moving economy into an absolute grinding halt. This is a national issue that impacts everyone's pocketbook no matter what stage of life's journey you are in.

My intention here is not to make a political statement. Rather I want to help my readers and clients to be fiscally responsible and make good financial decisions during each phase of their life.

In this column, I have touched on financial issues for young adults during college and the early years as they launch their careers. Over the years, I have written numerous articles targeted to families during their prime working years. These articles have dealt with everything from mortgages, saving for college and investing for retirement.

I have also endeavored to help people during the latter years of their careers. Those articles have discussed various aspects of Social Security issues and the loss of a spouse, and contained a number of tips for preparing for retirement.

The common thread of my articles geared to the early, middle and golden years, has been the stability of the United States financial system.

Although our nation is considered the gold standard of the world, we shouldn't simply assume it will continue to be in the years ahead.

A major ratings agency downgraded our debt rating from AAA to AA+. While that's still considered outstanding, it's not the absolute best. And I don't believe our ballooning debt can continue to be ignored.

But though I'm alarmed about our nation's spending habits, I remain confident about our nation's financial future. I say this because we have a history of overcoming adversity. Unfortunately, in this instance, it's self-inflicted.

We aren't alone. Currently, there are economic concerns in a number of countries throughout the world. But I feel that we have both the talent and resources to lead by example.

If we get our spending issues under control and the debt line trending downward, we'll have a more stable economy. Our fear and uncertainty will be replaced with stability and confidence. And a confident America will thrive and prosper.

1 - As of June 20th, the U.S. national debt was **$14,344,524,186,068.19**.

2 - 30 years ago, the U.S. national debt was approximately 14 times smaller.

3 - It took from the presidency of George Washington to the presidency of Ronald Reagan for the U.S. government to accumulate one trillion dollars of debt.

4 - Since then, we have added more than 13 trillion dollars of additional debt.

5 - The United States government is responsible **for more than a third** of all the government debt in the entire world.

6 - If you divide up the national debt equally among all U.S. households, each one owes over **$125,000**.

Ken Morris
As seen in The Oakland Press 12/23/12

Commitment to saving and investing crucial to your finances.

This is not only the time of year to get together with family and friends, it's also the opportune time to step up and help those that are not quite as fortunate.

Yes, I realize that many people need help each and every day, but in the spirit of the season, it would be nice to do a little bit extra this year. The Salvation Army bell ringers and the Toys for Tots programs are wonderful examples of helping out during the holiday season.

In my mind's calendar, time is passing by much too quickly. Not very long ago, I was stunned when I walked out of the grocery store and heard the bell ring. How suddenly the holiday season began! It seems like just two or three weeks ago that I was cheering for the Tigers in the World Series. Now, I 'm scrambling to shop and wrap Christmas presents.

Generally speaking, and barring an end of year financial melt-down, 2012 surprised a lot of people in a positive way. As I recall, plenty of pundits were predicting doom and gloom for 2012. But on the whole, it looks to me like it will turn out to be a fairly decent year.

Looking ahead to 2013, many seem to be expressing the same kind of skepticism they had for 2012. I can understand the negativity because we're a divided country with a great number of financial issues and problems that simply are not being addressed realistically.

People ask me all the time what they need to do to put themselves in a position to have enough money in retirement. I like to remind them that I don't have a crystal ball. But based on years of experience working with successful retirees, I can share the common thread of success.

Just as I was, my retired clients and many others are amazed at how fast father time passes by. But my observation regarding retirees who are successful at wealth accumulation is not that they were better than others at investing.

Rather, they chose to invest regardless of the headlines and worries of the day. In other words, they stayed with their game plan. They didn't stop investing because of worrisome events like the Cold War and civil unrest issues of the 1960s.

They stuck to their commitment to invest during the oil embargo of the 1970s. They didn't abandon their plan and quit investing when the market fell 20 percent in one day in 1987.

And once again proving that strategic investment requires an iron will, they stayed the course after we were attacked on September 11, 2001.

The future will always be filled with uncertainty. Often times, the world just doesn't make sense, and it's easy to develop a negative mindset. Successful investors don't let that happen.

Life is full of unexpected twists and turns that we simply cannot control. My best advice is to continue with your commitment to save and invest. That's something you can control.

On a more personal note, I would like to wish all my readers a very Merry Christmas. The holidays are a time to especially enjoy your friends and family. As you share those good times, I hope you will also remember those that are less fortunate.

Ken Morris
As seen in Oakland Press 6/29/14

Want to enjoy retirement? Plan on it.

Many readers are preparing to travel during the July 4th holiday. As people pull up to the pumps to fill their tanks, there will probably be a lot of grumbling over the price of a gallon of gasoline. Some will blame big oil for the rising cost; some will blame the never-ending crisis in the Middle East; and others will blame the government.

In recent years, it seems like one of the most popular words in our nation's vocabulary is "blame." Over the years, I have observed that blaming someone or something for a problem is much easier than trying to find a workable solution.

I have also concluded that, in most instances, including financial issues, making decisions during times of high stress seldom leads to viable long-term solutions.

Shortly after I graduated from high school in the 1970s, I heard quite a few politicians and business leaders talk about the need for a national energy policy. The need is certainly real, but the ability of politicians to make hard choices appears to be non-existent.

Here we are forty years later and our nation still does not have any semblance of an energy policy. Essentially, there nothing but a wild mishmash of federal and state rules and regulations without any coordinated goals or objectives. This is called winging it.

There are a lot of parallels that can be drawn between a national energy policy and retirement planning. I am certain that there are many individuals out there who entered the workforce between forty and fifty years ago, and who have no real retirement plan today. What they might have are a few 401(k) programs, a couple of IRAs and a few dollars in the bank.

They likely have no stated income goal, nor, in all probability, any rhyme or reason as to how their investments are allocated. In other words, their retirement planning never had a plan. It just evolved into a nest egg that they hoped would carry them through their retirement years.

They, too, are winging it as they go. When they reach retirement, you are likely to hear a lot of blaming others for their financial issues. In their minds, their own lack of planning and goal setting had nothing to do with their dire straits. Unfortunately, this is exactly like us not having a national energy policy.

For years, famous oilman T. Boone Pickens has made appearances on a number of news shows preaching the importance of a national energy policy. He has spent a lot of his own money in order to spread the message.

A nation having a viable energy policy is similar to an individual having an intelligent financial plan. Both require diversification, risk management and stated, measurable goals and objectives. Insofar as establishing an energy policy, our politicians have failed to do so, in spite of the fact that they've been aware of the need since the oil crisis in the mid-seventies.

But there's nothing keeping you from instituting a simple household financial plan. It's far better than flying by the seat of your pants, and it helps to organize and achieve stated goals. Don't let the lack of a plan lead the blame game. If you have no plan, you know where the blame belongs.

Ken Morris
As seen in Oakland Press 1/18/15

How many baskets are your eggs in?

Over the years I have frequently stated that most investors would be well served by maintaining a diversified portfolio. While I am certainly not alone in this opinion, I want to highlight exactly why I'm a strong proponent of diversification.

First, I have to acknowledge that some investors have indeed made a lot of money by focusing their investment dollars into one category, such as stocks or real estate. Others have garnered significant returns by putting all their money into just one stock.

So, yes, there is the potential to make a lot of money by putting all your investing dollars into a narrow category. But there is also significantly more risk.

Throughout my career, I don't believe there's a point of view I haven't heard. One good example is real estate. How many times have you heard the "experts" claim that you could never lose money in real estate?

Recent history has proven that opinion inaccurate as both commercial and residential real estate have actually decreased in value. Unfortunately, many people learned the hard way by not only losing money, but also their residence.

It was sad and expensive lesson, but it did conclusively prove that real estate values could fluctuate.

Gold is another poster child for fluctuation. For a long time infomercials flooded the airwaves advising everyone to buy gold for portfolio stability.

But it wasn't stable. It's down substantially, whether it was purchased in its physical form or as a stock or ETF. And investors who bought at the peak are a long way from getting their heads above water.

Another commodity that's dramatically plummeted in market value is oil. If you invested in oil, you're very likely to be hurting real bad at the moment. My condolences.

Most investors are aware of the inherent risk in stocks. In the 1950's GM President Charles Wilson stated, "...because for years I thought what was good for the country was good for General Motors and vice versa." At the time GM had an aura around it much as Apple does today.

Unfortunately, far too many people had a significant percentage of their nest egg tied up in GM stock. I'm not trying to pick on GM, but it is further substantiation that it's inherently risky to put all your eggs in one basket.

Locally, there are two recent examples that even bonds carry risk. Going back to GM, during the bankruptcy bondholders who thought they were first in line took a back seat to the unions. And when the City of Detroit went bankrupt, city bondholders also took a significant hit.

I don't want to come off as sounding like a purveyor of doom and gloom, but the point is, to a certain degree, everything carries an element of risk. Most investors would be better served being diversified not only among various asset classes, but also diversified within each class.

For example, in a category such as domestic stocks, rather than putting the entire amount into just ABC stock, consider adding DEF. And maybe even XYZ as well.

Simply stated, in our unpredictable, constantly changing economic environment, I firmly believe that most investors will be better served in the long term by utilizing a well-balanced, diversified portfolio. But even that requires periodic review and modifications.

Ken Morris
As seen in Oakland Press 1/24/16

How to be certain in uncertain times.

The new year has not been kind to investors. In fact, to put it bluntly, it's been downright brutal from the very start. The only bright spot is that we know what fueled the sudden downturn. Just take a look at what's going on around the world.

There were the North Koreans testing a nuclear weapon. Or at they're claiming to. In China, a steadily sagging economy is perpetuating a staggering slide in their stock market. And in the rarely stable

Middle East, tensions remain high between Iran and Saudi Arabia.

All this uncertainty has spurred an economic slowdown, which, in turn, has lead to dramatic drops in commodity prices. Oil prices have been the most visible; we see them every day at the pumps. But copper and steel have also taken terrific tumbles.

Yes, there's no doubt about it. The world has been dealing with an onslaught of unsettling news.

In the midst of the uncertainty, there is a bit of good news. At least domestically. Our own auto companies are reaching unprecedented heights. In 2015, car sales were 17.5 million. While it wasn't by much, it was enough to break the record of 17.4 million set in 2000. But bright spots notwithstanding, the pervasive mood is still one of caution and apprehension.

As a financial advisor who has guided many households through unsettling times, I suggest everyone keep a level head. Yes, it's upsetting to see your daily account values tumble, but changing your financial course in the middle of a downturn may hurt your nest egg in the long run.

Of course, you could sell all your investments now and buy them back when things get better. But while this strategy may work for a rare few, in my experience not many investors ever get it right on both ends. They typically sell at the bottom and re-enter near the top.

Most are better served by developing a diversified strategy and maintaining it throughout economic cycles. Generally, it's a good idea leave things to the money managers you had confidence to manage your funds in the first place

They follow your investments and the economic climate daily, affording them the opportunity to jump on opportunities that can add to the value of your portfolio.

Unfortunately, in the investment world it's too easy to pull the plug on your well-thought-out plans. More often than not bad things happen when fear takes control.

Imagine you're on a commercial flight and your plane suddenly encounters some severe turbulence. Would you consider asking the pilot if you could take over and land the plane?

That doesn't make any sense, but that's exactly what some are doing with their money. Modifications in your portfolio may be appropriate during a review. Tweaking a portfolio periodically may be in order. But total abandonment? It seldom turns out good.

Abandoning your strategy may make you feel better initially. But in the long term, the odds are your nest egg will suffer. I understand that it's difficult to see account values fall. But I'm confident that investors who stick with their strategy will be rewarded for their commitment.

I don't know when the slide will stop or the market will turn around. But I do know both events will happen.

Ken Morris
As seen in Oakland Press 5/21/17

The financial ramifications of being a Baby Boomer.

From a political standpoint, our nation is extremely divided. People are very outspoken about their opinions, and anyone with a different worldview or interpretation of topics is either ostracized or vilified.

Unfortunately, listening appears to be a lost art. And adult discussions regarding current events seem to be a thing of the past.

That being said, Baby Boomers, those born between 1946 and 1964, comprise nearly one-third of our population. If that's you, you especially need to pay attention to your finances.

Every day for the next fifteen years, a Baby Boomer will turn 65. Politics aside, there are certain things you need to know, whether you're liberal, conservative or somewhere in between.

If you're currently in the workforce you need to know that you're permitted extra contributions into your retirement programs. In 2017, everyone over age 50 is allowed an additional $6,000 contribution into their 401(k) or 403(b) for a total of $24,000. For an IRA, those 50 or older can deposit an extra $1,000.

Boomers also need to know that they can begin taking penalty-free withdrawals form their retirement accounts at age 59½. Naturally, there are taxes due on such withdrawals, unless the account is a Roth IRA. In that case, taxes have already been paid.

Then there's Social Security. You can begin receiving reduced benefits as early as 62. Should you? That's one of the most important financial decisions a household ever has to make. It's quite complex, and I recommend that most Boomers seek professional advice prior to making that decision.

If you were born between 1943-54, your full retirement age for Social Security is 66. And that number increases to the point that someone born in 1960 or later doesn't reach full retirement until age 67.

Those already collecting Social Security are automatically en-rolled for both Parts A and B of Medicare. If you're not currently col-lecting Social Security, you should still claim your Medicare benefits three months prior to reaching your 65th birthday.

Enrolling for Medicare is only part of the equation, however. Shopping for an appropriate supplement is critical and it may take a significant amount of time to find one that's appropriate. Your health history, of course, is the key.

Finally, Boomers need to be aware of the Required Minimum Distribution (RMD). You must take distributions from your retirement accounts no later than the April 1 of the year after you reach age 70½.

Clearly, Boomers need to know about their finances, regardless of political leanings. In the U.S. money is green and it's accumulated by your own work, saving and investing. It's not blue or red and it has no political leanings.

Consider this column a sort of Cliff's Notes reminder of the things that Boomers need to know. To say that our tax code is overly com-plex is an understatement. Consequently, there are exceptions to al-most everything I just addressed. And that means you will likely have to do some in-depth research.

Paying attention to your nest nest egg requires keeping a close eye on the intricacies of government-administered programs. When to tap your nest egg, at what age to collect Social Security and what kind of Medicare supplement to buy are all issues Baby Boomers need to address. I sincerely hope you do.

CHAPTER 9

Role-models. Maybe you have more.

Ken Morris
As seen in The Oakland Press 11/13/11
Many changes coming for retirees.

Years ago, I had the privilege of hosting a seminar in which Art Linkletter was the featured speaker. For my younger readers, Art Linkletter was a pioneer in television, an innovation that was considered quite a technological breakthrough at the time,

I could spend hours writing about Mr. Linkletter, but I just want to refer to a phrase he was known for: "Old age is not for sissies." As life expectancies continue to increase, the definition of "old age" continues to rise.

There are a lot of changes in the works for 2012 that will impact people that are already retired as well as those that are still working and preparing for retirement.

Beginning in 2012, the fifty-five million who are receiving Social Security benefits will see their benefit increase for the first time since 2009. The increase amounts to 3.6 percent. According to the Social Security Administration, this amounts to $43 more per month for the "average" retiree.

The eight million people who are recipients of the Supplemental Security Income program will also receive the 3.6 percent increase.

For those still in the workforce, the amount withheld from their paychecks for Social Security taxes in 2010 was reduced from 6.2 percent to 4.2 percent. The intent of the one-year reduction was to put more money into the consumers' pockets in the hope of getting the economy moving again.

At this point in time, it's slated to go back to the 6.2 percent level. I wouldn't be surprised, however, if the politicians step in at the 11th hour and maintain the 4.2 percent.

Regardless of whether the Social Security payroll tax withheld is at 4.2 percent or 6.2 percent, about 10 million Americans will see their Social Security tax increase.

That's because the amount of income subject to Social Security taxation for those still working increases from $106, 800 to $110,100. As it stands now, this amounts to an annual tax increase of just over $200 for both the employee and the employer.

That's not an enormous increase, but compare the number to the tax rates of the Clinton era. In 2000, the last full year of his Presidency, the maximum income subject to Social Security taxation was $76,200. So the Social Security payroll tax burden has definitely increased significantly since 2000.

For those that are working and looking to sock away a bit more in their 401(k) program, the allowable amount has increased by $500 to $17,000 annually.

Art Linkletter was right when he said old age wasn't for sissies. I would also like to add that preparing for retirement isn't for sissies either. If you're still working, don't put off saving and investing for retirement. The time will arrive much sooner than you realize. Remember, the retirement years can easily represent one-third of your life.

If you're already retired, you especially need to stay on top of the financial game. You can't just ride into the sunset without a worry in the world.

The financial rules seem to constantly change. Seniors not only have to deal with the ever-changing money issues, but they also have to sort through the complexity of Medicare coverage.

Ken Morris
As seen in Oakland Press 8/3/14

Invest like an astronaut.

Just a little over 45 years ago, I was on vacation with my family at a cottage on Wamplers Lake in the Irish Hills, not far from Ann Arbor. I watched along with the rest of the world as our nation's astronauts stepped onto the moon. What an amazing and historic accomplishment!

Perhaps I was just young and naïve, but I was excited and proud of our nation. Our president had set a goal when we fell behind the space race after the Soviet Union launched Sputnik.

By landing on the moon, we showed the world that we're a nation of doers and were up to virtually any challenge. It was a combination of technology, hard work and risk. In my humble opinion, we have drifted away from being a nation of innovation and risk and become more a nation of complacency.

Along with the rest of the world, we have witnessed dramatic changes since we landed on the moon. Technology has simply changed the way we live. Our daily lives now include cell phones and computers that are well beyond the technology used in the space programs that took us to the moon. Today, we tend to take all of this technology for granted.

Somehow, during the past 45 years, we moved from a nation of calculated risk takers that made the United States great, to one that is very risk averse.

Why? Perhaps it's because taking on risk usually means there are winners and losers, and in today's world, society doesn't want anyone to be a loser. For example, in many youth sports, everyone gets a medal or a trophy. Often times the score isn't even kept.

I bring this up because long-term investors require the kind of

155

mental makeup displayed by those space program pioneers of 45 years ago. When you move forward, some setbacks are probable. But you need to keep moving forward until you attain your goal.

Dangerous situations need to be respected, but they shouldn't bring progress to a grinding halt. The United States has never shied away from risk and tackling insurmountable goals. After all, this is the place where dreams come true.

And yet, investors tend to forget that owning a stock actually does represent ownership. When you own a company, there are ups and downs, setbacks and successes. There are often factors out of your control that can impact your company. In other words, owning something usually carries an element of risk.

Today, there are conflicts all over the world. It's quite unsettling and somewhat frightening. But investors, like space explorers, need to know how to handle risk. You cannot ignore it; you have to maintain focus on your established goals and objectives.

I've often said that investors need iron stomachs. But in addition, they have to be able to keep their emotions at arm's length. When you own a business, there are always issues and obstacles to overcome. And, as a stockholder, you do own a business.

That's why you need to invest like an astronaut. Be aware that there's an element of risk. Understand that periodic setbacks are likely to occur. And most important, maintain focus on your financial goals. If you can manage to do all that, the sky's the limit.

Ken Morris
As seen in Oakland Press 8/17/14

How to save like a hero.

Being a financial advisor isn't just a job; I also consider it to be a lifestyle. It's an occupation that requires one to be a technician and also to have the skills to interact with people. For me, it's a badge I carry proudly and enjoy thoroughly.

I periodically attend education conferences that help me stay current with investment trends, economic forecasts, and the onslaught of new and constantly changing rules and regulations. There's no question that the variety of classes is valuable, but what I find even more valuable is what I learn from my peers from other parts of the country and from the featured speakers from outside our profession.

My most recent seminar was in Nashville. It featured two outstanding speakers: Marcus Luttrell and Chesley "Sully" Sullenberger. Lutrell was a Navy Seal from Texas who survived Operation Red Wings on the slopes of Sawtalo Sar, a mountain in Afghanistan. He was the only survivor of the mission and his book, *Lone Survivor*, was made into a movie. His talk was intense and from the heart.

Sullenbeger, the other featured speaker, was also quite newsworthy. He was the pilot who landed his passenger jet on the Hudson River when it lost all engines due to a bird strike shortly after takeoff. His ability to bring the aircraft down safely was truly incredible and witnessed as it happened on national television. Sully spoke with the eloquence of a college professor.

In many ways the speakers were complete opposites. Marcus was a fairly young man with young children. Sully, on the other hand, has grown children and was near the end of his career when he piloted the aircraft to a safe landing. They were total opposites in their backgrounds and education.

So why mention these guys in a financial column? Because of what they shared in common, something of value to all people, including investors. Years and years of training that helped them survive.

For Marcus, it was physical Navy Seal training that pushed his body to the limits. For Sully, it was the technical training of a pilot. Sully pointed out that flight simulators didn't have water landings, but his many years of training simply kicked in during the time of crisis.

As investors, we may not need the physical toughness of a Navy Seal, but we do need to have the mental training. For example, you can mentally train yourself to be a saver. And maintain that mindset regardless of the financial circumstances.

A person that deposits a dollar in a piggybank every day is a simple example. So is someone that contributes every payday into his or her retirement plan.

It's easy to find a reason not to save. But with strong financial discipline and the ability to keep emotions in check, anyone can do it. You just have to train yourself to act that way.

If either Marcus or Sully had panicked in their situations, they would not have survived. I have written many times that investors need to keep their emotions at bay. In most instances, if you panic and make emotional decisions with your money, you lose.

As an investor, you need to be mentally tough and keep your emotions in check. All it takes is the proper training.

Ken Morris
As seen in Oakland Press 4/30/17

Are we teaching our children enough about finances?

One of the things I enjoy most about my profession is helping clients achieve and maintain their financial goals. Typically, the most significant goal is a financially stress free retirement.

One of my concerns is when clients put their own financial future in jeopardy by assisting a family member for a non-essential item with no real chance of being repaid. Of course, it's their money and they can do with it what they want, but family members sometimes take advantage of a big heart.

A few weeks ago, I saw a quote from former Notre Dame football coach Lou Holtz hanging on the wall in a restaurant. It said, "In the nineties, everybody wants to talk about their rights and privileges. Twenty-five years ago, people talked about their obligations and responsibilities."

Yes we're well beyond the 1990s, but I believe what he said is still very much applicable as it relates to money. I'm all in favor of those that are financially comfortable assisting family members when it's appropriate and affordable.

Contributing to a grandchild's college savings fund or helping a son or daughter with a loan or gift are legitimate reasons to dip into your nest-egg, especially if you're confident about your own financial future.

That being said, I also believe we're shielding our young ones from financial reality. Is the cost of higher education is too high? Absolutely. But instead of addressing the cause, student loans have ballooned and many are in default. And if you're among those who want it to be free, I wouldn't hold my breath.

Health care is another issue. Having children on their parents' policy until age 26 may be beneficial for mom and dad. But again, I question whether we're shielding our young adults from financial reality and maybe even coddling them.

Without question there are many people who truly need financial assistance. But then there are those who feel they're entitled to a middle-class lifestyle without exerting any effort. They don't share the responsibility and work ethic that many have put forth in order to achieve middle-class status. Middle class is not an entitlement; it's an accomplishment.

Hard work, study, saving, sacrifice and commitment are all common traits I see in financially successful clients. When they tell me stories about their successful grandchildren, it's obvious that they also possess these attributes.

But when they share stories about their struggling kids or grandkids, the issue usually seems to be lack of motivation and direction. When it comes to finances, you have to wonder at what age someone should be considered an adult.

For some time, I have been a proponent of financial education beginning as early as middle school. As parents, I believe we continually need to help our children and grandchildren get a grasp on finances.

Sometimes the lessons may be painful, but one can often learn more from adversity, or difficult and uncomfortable situations, than they can from having a smooth, worry free journey.

In the real world, not everybody gets a trophy. Rewards are far more meaningful when they're won, not just handed to someone because they participated. Don't be afraid to say no to a loved one asking for money. In the long run, you just might be doing them a favor.

Ken Morris
As seen in Oakland Press 5/6/18

There's a difference between listening and hearing.

I recently attended a convention in Arizona with many of America's leading financial advisors. One of the featured speakers was Alan Mulally, the former Chief Executive Officer of Ford Motor Company.

As you would expect, he discussed his past leadership positions with both Boeing and Ford. After listening to him speak, I believe the reason he succeeded at both corporations was his ability to really listen.

He made it a point to get a firm grasp of the issues and discuss the facts with both his management team and union leaders. Only then did he make decisions that he thought were best for each company. Clearly, his approach was successful.

Over the years I've crossed paths with a lot of successful business managers. Without exception, they were well educated, and in most instances, had great knowledge of their industry.

But that wasn't the case with Mr. Mulally. His background wasn't automotive at all; it was in aerospace. During his presentation, it occurred to me that the common thread among the successful people in attendance wasn't just their knowledge. It was also their ability to listen to others and reflect on their perspectives.

Too often, I believe, people listen with the intent of determining how they will respond. They listen without hearing, concentrating more on providing a rationale for their own opinion or viewpoint. I feel this lack of real listening is very evident in today's politics. It's not surprising we're so divided as a nation.

When it comes to managing your money, listening and gathering information is also imperative. A lot of bad money decisions are made because people don't fully analyze the data they've gathered. Or perhaps they only hear what they want to hear.

Who among us hasn't been bombarded with advertisements on radio, television and on-line streaming? We've all heard car ads telling us we can drive a beautiful new car for just $199 per month. But maybe we don't hear that the price only applies if you limit your driving to 10,000 miles per year. That's a problem if your daily commute is 50 miles round trip. To effectively manage your money, you can't just hear; you have to analyze and understand.

Similarly, successful financial advisors need to have broad knowledge in a world where tax laws continually change; where financial issues across the globe can impact financial outcomes right here at home; and where many financial transactions utilize plastic instead of cash.

The fact is that the financial world is far more complex today than it was just a few years ago. And in addition to being on top of the constantly changing financial milieu, financial advisors also need to listen and understand the complexities of each individual and his or her family history.

Are there health issues? Is there a family member with special needs? Is it a blended family? What are their retirement dreams?

In other words, a good financial advisor not only has to grasp the intricacies and emotions of each household, but also the complexities of the financial world.

Successful advisors know how to listen and lead their clients through the onslaught of advertisements, politics and daily events. Mr. Mulally is a great example of how real listening can help lead us through these turbulent times.

CHAPTER 10

Advice to Young,

Ken Morris
As seen in Oakland Press 7/20/14

The benefits of education vs. the cost of education.

It's hard to believe that school starts up again in a matter of weeks. While I can't overemphasize the importance of education, I believe today's young adults face quite a juggling act in the years ahead.

Statistics demonstrate just how important education is to one's lifetime earnings. On the other hand, graduating from college with large student loans can be devastating to one's finances.

The juggling act of getting an education and minimizing debt is a major challenge. Nonetheless, I was astonished at the Washington Center for Equitable Growth's report that there are 5.8 million young people that are either not enrolled in school or not working. I don't know how they will ever become financially self sustaining.

For those aged 16 to 24, the unemployment rate is roughly double the national average. Narrowing the category to ages 16 to 19, unemployment is approaching 25 percent.

One ticket out of unemployment is education. According to the Bureau of Labor Statistics, if you have less than a high school education, unemployment is nearly twenty percent.

With a high school diploma the rate falls to fifteen percent. With some college, it goes down to roughly twelve percent, and with a Bachelors degree or higher, it drops dramatically to just over five percent.

Clearly, education reduces the likelihood of unemployment, but college debt still remains an obstacle. Without education there's little work, but without work, how can you pay for an education? It's indeed a major problem.

As a financial advisor, I believe it's extremely important that people understand the mathematics of life. A borrower should understand how much it really costs to pay back a debt. A saver and investor should take the time to understand how much they need to save and invest to reach their financial goals.

Likewise, young adults need to understand that, if they want to get ahead in this competitive world, that they truly need to educate themselves. They need to learn to manage both money and debt, and develop a strong work ethic.

Over the years, I've found statistics can be misleading. People, especially politicians, tend to twist numbers to fit their agendas. I recently came across a statistic regarding young people living in their parents' homes that I consider misleading on.

The official census states that half of those under 25 live with their parents. That sounds like doom and gloom for young people.

But then the Census Bureau states, "It is important to note that the Census Population Survey counts students living in dormitories as living in their parents' home."

I think this is extremely important because the number of young adults in college has actually been increasing at a steady rate since the 1980s. In other words, what statistics show on the surface appears to be doom and gloom, but in reality, is good news.

Many young adults are not rotting away in their parents' basement, but rather are crammed into dorm rooms trying to improve their lot in life. True, they might be in the dorms on mom and dad's money, but they're not in basements, as the statistics would lead you to believe.

The bottom line is to get a good, practical education and try to minimize debt. And enjoy your college years; the real world comes soon enough.

Ken Morris
As seen in Oakland Press 9/7/14

It's not too late to "Go West!"

Summer vacations can be both fun and educational. My recent western states vacation is a good example. When I head for the west coast, I generally make several stops. One of the most interesting was at Rapid City, SD.

To my surprise, the city has life size bronze statues of all our presidents. I wandered into the main office and learned that the artists and statues were funded and maintained by a private organization. A gentleman explained to me that it was their way of honoring our nation.

My next stop was the Mount Rushmore National Memorial, where I was fascinated to learn the process of its dream, design, construction and ongoing maintenance. It's also where I decided the direction of today's column.

I overheard some startling comments from the large contingent of domestic and foreign visitors, including such as "Who is that along with Washington and Lincoln?" But my favorite was "Why did they put Roosevelt on the monument before he was president?" Obviously, some visitors were confusing Teddy and Franklin D.

Whenever I turned on the news during my western trip, the topic was Ferguson, MO, just outside of St. Louis. In our nation's history, St. Louis was the starting point for many western settlers.

Most were seeking the American Dream of a better economic life. People have continually moved west seeking a better lifestyle. Those journeys were not without risk, and, on some occasions, ended in death.

The nation has changed dramatically since the Wild West was settled. While the American Dream is still alive and well, I fear that many don't share the dream or simply lack the drive to improve their lot in life.

As a financial advisor, I help people handle their finances. Except for the few that inherited their wealth, most accumulate it through work and investment. But the foundation for building wealth is something that many seem to be lacking.

Our nation's challenge is to develop new opportunities that lead to good jobs and careers. I believe we need a modern-day western journey to revive the American dream. In other words, we should be emphasize having dreams and taking calculated risks rather than debating the minimum wage.

It appears our focus is on just getting by rather than aiming for the sky. My youngest son and some of his friends are good examples. After graduating from college at the height of the recession he "went west."

He discovered there are plenty of well-paying jobs for those that are willing to dedicate themselves and work hard. Many in his age group followed the same path.

In the investment world, you need to find the balance between minimizing risk and maximizing aggressiveness. I don't mean if you're without work or unhappy with your job, that you should drop everything and head west tomorrow. But you shouldn't abandon your dreams.

There are indeed many opportunities that can be pursued. The American Dream that pushed many of our forefathers west still exists. You might have to look a bit harder to find them, but they are out there. Our history is full of stories of individuals who took risk and found success. America has changed, but with hard work, a bit of risk and maybe a little luck, no dream is unattainable.

Ken Morris
As seen in Oakland Press 10/1/17

The journey of a lifetime.

This past summer, one of my many cousins organized a family reunion. It was nice to catch up with so many of my aunts, uncles and cousins. One of my cousins is a rocket scientist who more than twenty years ago was instrumental in the launch of Cassini, the spacecraft that was sent to orbit Saturn.

In mid September, my cousin sent everyone in the family an email reminding us that after its seven-year trip to Saturn and thirteen years in orbit, the mission was coming to an end because the Cassini was, in essence, out of fuel. My cousin was proud, as he should have been, because he was at the Jet Propulsion Lab from beginning to end.

I'm no rocket scientist, but just like my cousin, I like to see things through to fruition. As a financial advisor, this entails a lifelong journey with families. I take great pride in the fact that most of my retired clients are financially comfortable.

My mission in assisting retirees to achieve their objective is being accomplished. Many are now at a stage in life where they want their adult children to meet me, my son who is a Certified Financial Planner and other key members of our staff.

They want them to know us because they're confident our firm can guide the next generation in setting and establishing goals and managing money. I believe such intergenerational meetings are definitely valuable.

First, it's important that those who will ultimately inherit know how their parents' nest egg was amassed. In one recent meeting, for example, the children seemed surprised at the size of their parents' portfolio.

I explained to them how it was built. I pulled out payroll stubs dating back to 1993, showing that one parent was saving eight percent of each paycheck and the other ten percent. I emphasized their commitment to saving no matter the economic situation.

Even during the college tuition years they continued to save. They amassed their sizeable nest egg by setting monies aside every paycheck. Nothing could derail their commitment. I've always maintained that a commitment to save and invest is more important than the actual choice of investment.

Another reason I think generational meetings are important is to remind the kids that when they inherit the nest egg, it's ok to change investments. They're not obligated to follow mom and dad's path.

In a recent meeting, one of my client's children was a real environmentalist. My son explained to her how the investment world has made numerous socially conscious investment choices available.

For example, if you don't want tobacco or alcohol stocks, no problem. If you prefer an investment that promotes clean water, there are plenty of them. Without going into a detailed explanation, your heirs don't have to maintain the same investments you selected.

The next generation may have completely different goals, passions and beliefs. In that respect, I'm pleased that the financial services industry can design a wide variety of socially responsible portfolios.

Financial advisors are here for the lifelong journey, from career launch, throughout the working career and into retirement years. Then it's time to help pass the baton to the next generation.

It may not be rocket science, but financial advising is a journey I have greatly enjoyed.

Ken Morris
As seen in Oakland Press 6/10/18

The student loan programs are failing.

There was recently an article in the well-respected Wall Street Journal that really upsets me. It bothers me as a taxpayer and concerns me even more as a financial advisor.

The article revealed some startling statistics garnered by the U. S. Department of Education. There are now more than 100 people that owe in excess of $1 million on their student loans.

What makes it even more staggering is that only five years ago there were just 14 people carrying a seven-figure debt load. Equally alarming is that 2.5 million people that still owe more than $100,000.

According to several sources, including the Federal Reserve Bank of New York, total student debt currently exceeds $1.4 trillion. Yes, trillion. The total number of student borrowers is more than 45 million. That's an incredible 70% of all college students.

As a financial advisor I can't help but ask myself how such a circumstance could arise. I'm not suggesting that student loans should be eliminated, but borrowers really need to calculate what it takes to repay the loan, including the interest.

Those numbers can balloon into an overwhelming financial burden. Because lenders are overly eager and generous and because students either don't calculate or understand what they're getting into, it looks like the taxpayers will be on the hook for a significant amount of the money owed.

As it currently exists, the student loan program simply is not working.

And the large number of student loan defaults is proof. By now, most high school seniors know where they'll be attending school in the fall. It will be the beginning of a journey that will entail many financial decisions along the way.

Unless a student has a full scholarship or a benefactor that can afford the enormous cost of higher education, it's likely that he or she will have to resort to getting loan.

But before anyone gets a student loan, I suggest they do the math. Just because you qualify for a loan doesn't mean you should rush to get one. There are several steps you can take to help avoid one, or at least to minimize the loan amount.

For example, instead of enrolling at the university of your dreams, take your prerequisite courses at a local and less expensive community college. Also make certain that, if you do get a loan, the money is used only for educational purposes. I fear that some borrowed monies end up on spring break trips. As much as I like a good time, I don't think vacations should be taken on Uncle Sam's dime.

I'm not pointing fingers, but the cost of education is escalating at an alarming rate. I have clients that, years ago, worked at auto plants over the summer and made enough to cover the next school year's expenses.

Granted, everything was cheaper back then, and since those days costs have escalated astronomically. Those high paying summer jobs are few and far between as well. It's no wonder the student loan programs are in such a mess today.

At the end of the day, we, as a nation need a viable solution that does not tie a financial anchor around a young person's ankles. Nor should any solution force the taxpayers to pay for a bailout.

Ken Morris
As seen in Oakland Press 12/9/18

An important takeaway from the California fires.

The fires in California were a real eye opener. It's hard to imagine that they came so incredibly fast people literally had to flee for their lives. Sadly, some didn't make it and many loved ones were separated in the confusion.

Most of us are used to observing orderly chaos due to the weather. How many times have we seen a state's governor urging people to flee from an incoming storm? Then watching them on the news boarding up their homes, loading their vehicles and joining miles-long traffic jams.

Maybe it is climate change, perhaps it's just the norm, but from a financial perspective, I believe every household needs to be prepared for a sudden and unexpected departure.

In other words, everyone should have a grab-and-go summary of important financial data along with some emergency cash.

I've always encouraged people to have concise documentation to guide their heirs if, God forbid, something unforeseen happens to them.

I mean a complete financial inventory to help them deal with and button up your finances.

The events in California highlighted why it's so essential to have a binder or a thumb drive with investment, banking and insurance information at your fingertips.

Many people have their credit card information and quite a bit of other important data on their telephone. But what if there's an issue with the electric grid? What if there's no cell service?

It's not my intent to promote doom and gloom or forecast the complete breakdown of our society. But we saw families flee their homes in an upscale community, and a few days later, living in tents. That's how quickly their lifestyle changed. They need emergency housing, clothing and some way to sustain themselves and begin rebuilding.

Businesses are in the same situation, including my own firm. Spurred on by the flooding in Houston, we installed an emergency plan to continue operation. If a disaster prevents us from getting into the office, we have a continuity plan in place that we periodically review and test.

How the members of our firm contact one another, access pertinent client data and communicate and service our clients are all part of the plan. Hopefully, we'll never need to implement it, but proper planning dictates that we be prepared.

At the household level, if you take the time to be organized for the benefit of your heirs, I suggest you help yourself and your immediate family members by taking it one step further.

Have critical information prepared so that you can quickly grab it if the circumstances dictate a sudden departure. An important element of your grab-and-go financial kit is establishing a family communication protocol.

For example, if you have an trusted friend or relative out of state, there should be standing instructions that everyone in your immediate family contact them to let them know where you are and that you're safe.

Our world is high tech. Our personal data is accessed through our smart phones and computers. Financial transactions are implemented with the click of a button or the swipe of a credit card. But if you suddenly need to flee and you temporarily can't access or utilize the data, you need a back-up financial plan.

The more complex our world becomes, the more you need to keep yourself organized.

Ken Morris
As seen in Oakland Press 1/20/19

A thought for your pennies.

Like so many sports fans, I watched a fair amount of football over the holidays. One advertisement that caught my eye was for a sports streaming service that lets you watch a game on your mobile device.

The visual for the commercial was a sports fan searching for loose change in his chair. The voiceover announcer stated that you could watch sports on your mobile device for "just 17 cents per day."

I thought the advertisement was well done and it made me smile. As a financial advisor, I can honestly say that, in and of itself, finding 17 cents isn't going to alter anyone's financial wellbeing.

But, let's not totally dismiss 17 cents per day. Using fourth grade math, 17 cents per day amounts to $62 per year. If you just dropped it into a piggy bank, you'd have $620 in ten years. I believe there are plenty of households right now that could put that money to good use.

The point is, when it comes to money, little things done consistently over a period of time add up to big things. Last year, I had a client meeting with a retired couple and their adult children. The objective was for the adult children to become familiar with their parents' finances and get to know me.

Both parents had good careers and contributed regularly to their employer sponsored retirement programs. The children saw the end of the story and were stunned. They wondered how mom and dad had amassed such a large nest egg.

I showed them old copies of their parents' paychecks. Over their work careers they had contributed a modest amount into their retirement every pay period. The accounts grew to a substantial sum.

The parents didn't stop participating when college tuition bills came due. Nor did the contributions stop for life event changes such as weddings, anniversaries or the birth of grandchildren.

They just kept feeding the piggy-bank year in and year out. That's the secret of building a truly significant nest egg. Consistent participation may even be more important than investment selection.

Here's a challenging for 2019. See how many ways you can find to feed your piggy bank. And I don't mean looking under your sofa seat cushions. Maybe it's nothing more than making your coffee at home rather than stopping in the coffee shop. Or it could simply be eating out less frequently.

More often than not, when people review their fixed spending, they can find places to shave more and redirect cash into savings. For example, raising the deductibles on your homeowner's insurance or better insulating your home. Things like that can add up over time.

Want a little fun? Take the double the penny challenge to jumpstart your savings. Start with one cent and every day double it. From one cent to two cents, from two cents to four cents and so on. It begins to get interesting in about two weeks. Let me know how far you get.

It's a great lesson in savings and learning the value of a dollar. Investments may go up and down but disciplined saving can be a constant. So get the basics down now. We have the rest of the year to tackle the complex world of planning and investing.

Ken Morris
As seen in the Oakland Press 3/24/19

These post-nuptial agreements make good financial sense.

It's an exciting weekend in the Morris household. My youngest son is getting married to a wonderful woman he met years ago in college.

Both have had good careers and each of them has done quite well financially, with a significant portfolio and money in the bank.

When I was married a lifetime ago, finances weren't a very big issue because there wasn't a lot of money to be concerned about. With my son and soon to be daughter-in-law, rather than calling it a wedding, I kiddingly refer to it as a merger.

Several weeks ago, they asked me how I thought they should handle their finances once they were married. There really is no right or wrong answer, but my feeling is that newlyweds should work toward consolidating their monies.

Rather than having two individually owned bank accounts, I believe that a married couple should work toward having just one. A joint account. I say this because if you can't be honest with one another about your money, there's a good chance your marriage is headed for trouble. Successful marriages are about openness, not keeping secrets from each other.

Merging investment accounts, on the other hand, is a little more difficult, primarily because of various issues regarding taxes.

Nonetheless, I believe these accounts should also be consolidated, even though it might take some time wading through paperwork.

Then there are retirement accounts, which have only one owner. I've often had to remind people that IRA stands for Individual Retirement Account, which means they can't be owned jointly. What you can do after getting married, however, is change the beneficiaries on all your IRA, 401(k) and 403(b) accounts.

If life insurance is part of either spouse's benefits package, the beneficiary designation should be changed to reflect the other spouse as beneficiary. Health insurance and other employer-sponsored benefits also need to be addressed. There is no mandated timetable to complete these tasks, but they should be taken care of before too long.

A few years ago, there was an article in one of my financial journals about a court case involving a deceased teacher. When he began his teaching career he was single and named a sibling as beneficiary on his retirement account. He later married and continued his career as an educator, contributing into his retirement account every pay period.

Unfortunately, he either forgot or never considered changing the beneficiary designation to his wife. When he passed away, she brought the matter to court because she felt the money rightfully belonged to her. But the court ruled in favor of the brother, the beneficiary of record.

That's why it's vital to make sure all your beneficiary designations are exactly the way you want them. Remember, even if you have a trust, your signed beneficiary designations with investment firms supersede the trust document.

In other words, when it comes to your finances, every minute detail should be considered and acted upon.

Over the course of a marriage, a lot of financial decisions will be made. I think it's best if you make them jointly. Many marriages falter due to financial disagreements. Based on my lifelong experience, this is often fueled by lack of communication. Most successful marriages feature couples that are open and plan their finances together.

Ken Morris
As seen in the Oakland Press 3/31/19

The best education money can buy?

One of the largest expenses a family will incur is very likely the cost of a child's education. To assist families with this financial responsibility, many programs that encourage saving are available.

The most common are the 529 college savings programs, which were originally intended specifically for post-high school studies. The newly implemented tax law, however, now allows them to help cover the cost of education prior to the college years.

Simply stated, the student is referred to as the beneficiary of the account. Any loved ones can contribute into the account, and 529 contributions grow tax-free. If used for a qualified educational expense, the monies come out of the account tax-free as well.

Clearly, the new legislation offers families several incentives to save for education. Most often, a parent or grandparent is the responsible party for the account. Generally, there is a large menu of investment choices from which you can select.

It's important to do your due diligence and research prior to making a commitment, because, as with any investment, it could decrease in value. On the surface, 529 accounts appear straightforward, but there are several investment firms offering programs, thereby adding to the complexity.

The high school years go by in the blink of an eye. Before you know it, there are ACT tests and college applications. More often than not it's a stressful process, especially if you have your heart set on just one or two schools.

Rejection is painful and no parents like to see their child hurt.

Parents can offer guidance and encouragement, cheer them on, or provide a shoulder to cry on. But at the end of the day, there is very little a parent can do to affect the outcome.

At least, that's what I thought. Then the recent headlines hit revealing the corruption of the college admission processes at what are considered elite universities.

Perhaps I'm naïve but I'm stunned at the magnitude of the corruption in college education admissions. The world is far from perfect, but pay-offs and bribes have no place in either the public or private sector.

I anticipate there will soon be more criminal charges. And don't be surprised if we soon hear that the IRS is taking a look at unreported income and financial transactions. I suspect this story will be in the news for some time to come.

I bring all this up in a financial column because I work day in and day out with families that want the best for their kids and grandkids. They save and invest, but they never cross the line called ethics. That's because they understand that achievements reached by cheating are hollow. And doors that are opened by money are likely to soon slam shut.

That being said, I'm a firm believer in networking. I'm frequently asked, "Who do you know?" or "What would you recommend?" Often as not, I suggest local chambers of commerce and civic organizations. They're great, legitimate places to meet people and open doors.

That's how relationships can be built and connections made that help beyond just the business world. What's unfolding before our eyes regarding college admissions is clearly wrong. In today's competitive world, education is important and expensive. But real education cannot be bought. It must be earned.